11-63

Alexander Hamilton's Pay Book

Edited by E. P. Panagopoulos

Department of History
San Jose State College

Detroit • Wayne State University Press • 1961

WAYNE STATE UNIVERSITY STUDIES · HISTORY · Number 10

E
302.6
.H2
A13
C.2

Published simultaneously in Canada by Ambassador Books, Limited,
Toronto, Ontario, Canada

Library of Congress Catalog Card Number 61-8641

*Grateful acknowledgment is made to the Ford Foundation for financial
assistance in the publication of this volume.*

Acknowledgements

I wish to express my appreciation to the staff of several libraries for the kind help they gave me during the preparation of this book: especially to Dr. David C. Mearns, Chief of the Manuscript Division of the Library of Congress, and the librarians of his division in the examination of the Alexander Hamilton manuscripts; to Dr. Henry J. Dubester, Chief of the General Reference and Bibliography Division of the same library, for expert bibliographical advice; and to Dr. G. Flint Purdy, Director, and Howard H. Lapham, Social Studies Librarian, of Wayne State University Libraries for valuable microfilms and access to a copy of the first edition of Postlethwayt's *Dictionary of Trade and Commerce.*

The following were generous and helpful in locating specific rare editions: R. N. Williams, Director, Historical Society of Pennsylvania; Edwin Wolf, Librarian, the Library Company of Philadelphia; James J. Heslin, Librarian, the New York Historical Society; Robert Rosenthal, Curator of Special Collections, the University of Chicago Library; and Clifford K. Shipton, Librarian, the American Antiquarian Society.

I am indebted to Mrs. Bernard Goldman, of Wayne State University, for many editorial suggestions and to Professor Benedict Einarson, of the University of Chicago, for giving me the benefit of his extensive knowledge on Plutarch. Professor George

Nakhnikian, Chairman, Department of Philosophy, Wayne State University, and Professor Harold C. Syrett, of Columbia University and Editor of *The Papers of Alexander Hamilton,* both read the last part of this volume and helped me greatly with their suggestions.

I wish particularly to express my gratitude to my teacher William Thomas Hutchinson, Sterling-Morton Professor of American History, University of Chicago, who read the greater part of the manuscript and criticized it; he has been a source of encouragement, guidance and inspiration. I alone am responsible, however, for whatever errors any readers may note, for these will be due to my own limitations.

E.P.P.

Contents

Introduction

The two parts of this book, the Notes and the brief study of certain philosophic premises of Alexander Hamilton, are related by the fact that both deal with the intellectual activity of the same man. Scholars have paid comparatively little attention to the philosophic aspect of Hamilton's life. Most research on him during the last 150 years has been concerned with the political, social, and economic relationships in which he was involved. And yet, if attention is focused only on these facets, no one can fully understand his many-sided life. Hamilton's intellectual activity was so intense and extensive that its exploration becomes necessary for the better understanding of his complex personality.

A completely different approach is that followed by several social scientists who replaced the political, social, and economic relationships of the eighteenth century with those of their own time. They placed him as hero or villain (depending on their individual preconceptions), in the midst of modern problems; and they made of Hamilton a symbol, something of what they cherished most, something of what they considered most wicked. Though one can understand this attitude, it is evident that scholarship profited very little from it.

After the analysis of the Notes new evidence came to light which may be helpful in clarifying a few obscure aspects of Hamilton's life. Particularly significant is the illumination of the problem of Hamilton's sources and his use of Postlethwayt's *The Universal Dictionary of Trade and Commerce*, a use not limited to the Notes only, but evident in some of Hamilton's major writings.

It is impressive, indeed, that a man with little formal education and with less than two years of college training was able to write such articulate and crystal-clear treatises on important economic, political, and military matters. These usually betray a broad knowledge of the subjects and a familiarity with authorities that had dealt with them previously. Even more impressive after reading his works is the pertinence of his proposed solutions and the forcefulness and freshness of his ideas. The question, therefore, of the sources of his information and the originality of his thought is a very interesting one.

The belief of some of his earlier admirers that Hamilton's ideas were original, that they sprang spontaneously from his genius, lost ground long ago. During the nineteenth century several scholars had pointed out the similarity of his economic thinking to British governmental practices of the eighteenth century. The likeness was obvious, and yet no one could establish a solid connection between them by pointing out Hamilton's actual sources. It is on this point that Postlethwayt's *Dictionary* has provided a missing link.

The significant role of Postlethwayt can be illustrated by the following example. It was in January 1790 that Hamilton for the first time stated in his well-known "First Report on the Public Credit" that "the proper funding of the present debt will render it a national blessing." He made this statement cautiously and was anxious to add that he was "far from acceding to the position, in the latitude in which it is sometimes laid down, that 'public debts are public benefits.'"

Though he himself implied that there were others before him who had thought in a similar way, his admirers coined the expression "a public debt is a national blessing," and thought of it as the most characteristic product of the Hamiltonian genius. What they admired most was the strong nationalistic implications of such a laconic statement on an economic policy. It might be frustrating for these uncritical admirers to find out that it was not Hamilton who was the originator of this phrase. Before him several British authorities had reached the same conclusion and had worded it in a similar manner. In 1748, an anonymous author of a pamphlet published in London and entitled *An Essay on Public Credit* affirmed that "it is to the national debt we owe our public credit"; and he proceeded to explain all the losses and inconveniences that would arise should the British government discharge the debt. The view of this pamphlet is further clarified by another anonymous author, who a year later published a tract under the title *Considerations upon a Reduction of the Land-Tax.* He explained that "war and expense are blessings, as they are the sources of debt: an enormous debt is a blessing, as it is the fountain of public credit."

This extreme view was not shared by everybody. Sir John Barnard, an esteemed public figure and a prolific writer of economic tracts, in his *Reasons for the More Speedy Lessening the National Debt,* published in 1737, remarked: "It is true, some modern politicians have run upon a notion, and several persons are weak enough to believe, that the not paying off the public debt will engage people the more to preserve the present government." However, the more Sir John advanced in age, the more he became "weak enough to believe" that there are certain benefits derived from a public debt. He said as much in *A Defence of Several Proposals for Raising Three Millions, . . .* published in 1746.

Thus, the several ideas that "the not paying off the public debt will engage people the more to preserve the present government," that a public debt is "a fountain of public credit," that a public debt is a "national" debt, and that the country is a "nation" had appeared in print at least fifty-three years earlier than 1790, when Hamilton wrote his "First Report on the Public Credit." The important point is that Hamilton had read them.

The above and many other authors and pamphlets are extensively quoted by Postlethwayt in the lengthy article "Funds," the material of which he repeated in the article "Credit" or "Public Credit." Hamilton quotes the article "Funds" in his Notes on pp. 242A and 243. It seems that years later, writing the statement on public credit, he went back and reread familiar passages from Postlethwayt.

It is only just to mention that Postlethwayt himself, being a spokesman of the British merchants, had violently attacked the idea that "the public debt is a national blessing." He thought that it "may be pretty amusement enough for stockmongers and usurers, over their cups, but a pernicious doctrine to be espoused and propagated by the sage statement." He also cautioned that the extinction of a public debt through a sinking fund or otherwise actually meant more taxes, which, of course, could be detrimental to the commercial interests of the country and could be a cause of general discontent. Thus, public credit could not really preserve the existing government. Concerning the relationship between the British monarch and the public debt, Postelthwayt again quotes Sir John Barnard, who had stated that "the throne of that prince, in a free nation, must be most firmly established, whose affairs will permit him to ask, or who desires to collect, the fewest taxes from the people." It is possible that it was Postelthwayt's strong opposition to the maintenance of a public debt that made Hamilton express his views cautiously.

This is only one example of how the Notes reveal Postelthwayt as one of the principal sources of Hamilton's economic writings. Study of the "Reports" offers more evidence of his use of Postelthwayt and helps in the clarification of the origin of some of Hamilton's ideas. He quotes many other authorities, classical and contemporary, in the Notes. On them, however, there are brief comments in the analysis of the text.

A complete evaluation of the Notes is almost impossible unless one considers their relationship to the pattern of Hamilton's thought. Only by doing so can one appreciate their significance in shaping his knowledge and ideas. Thus, for example, if the study of his works makes clear his preference for empirical knowledge rather than metaphysically rational knowledge, then the accumulation of all the empirical data in the Notes acquires an additional importance. An examination of the same data from the point of view of the significance attributed to them by Hamilton helps to clarify his empiricism. It is evident then that the study of certain philosophic premises of his thought becomes necessary.

Unfortunately, a small group of historians who reject an association of anything philosophic with Alexander Hamilton would react against such an examination. The cause of it is the sclerotic tradition of approaching Hamilton exclusively through certain relationships and the fact that a few historians still cling to a set of preconceptions. The objection that is usually raised is that since Hamilton was not a philosopher, how can one discuss his philosophic system.

If one could have asked Hamilton the flattering question, "Are you a philosopher?" it is almost certain that, despite the vanity attributed to him, he would have answered with an emphatic "No!" He might have admitted that he was a lawyer, or a man of military and political affairs, or even an *homme de lettres,* but philosopher, never! And it seems that no student of Hamilton's life has a different idea.

The viewpoint becomes different, however, when in the process of an examination of Hamilton's mind certain intellectual trends become evident and a developing pattern of thought emerges. It then becomes interesting to examine this pattern of thought in the light of the philosophic climate of his milieu. The fact that certain of his philosophic premises thus become clear does not mean either that he was a philosopher or that this is an attempt to make him appear to be one. Such an inquiry simply leads to conclusions which are of help in reaching a more profound understanding of the man. More than this, the same conclusions added to similar studies on Thomas Jefferson, Benjamin Franklin, and a few other distinguished men of their era can illuminate the Age of Enlightenment in America, an age that is inadequately understood.

The reader who is particularly interested in the "Pay Book" Notes may be surprised by the discussion of certain of Hamilton's philosophic premises, since they do not seem to be directly related to the Notes. However, both the Notes and the discussion contribute to a fuller understanding of Hamilton's thought. The Notes reveal his early interests, and his concern with empirical data suggests the direction of his subsequent intellectual development. The essay that follows the examination of the Notes, based upon his own works and correspondence, is an analysis of the thought of the mature Hamilton. Together they help clarify some of the basic tenets of one of America's most controversial figures.

1

Origin and Background of the Paybook

August of 1776 was a busy month for Alexander Hamilton.*
Five months earlier he had been appointed by the New York
Provincial Congress, Captain of the Artillery Company of that
Colony.[1] This company existed, however, only on paper. It was
Hamilton's duty to find, enlist, and equip his men, drill them daily
in the fields, and solve all the problems involved in the organiza-
tion and training of a new unit.[2]

---

* Part of this section appeared in my article "Hamilton's Notes in his
Pay Book of the New York State Artillery Company," *The American Historical Review*, LXII (1957) 310–25.

1. Berthold Fernow, ed., *Documents Relative to the Colonial History of
the State of New York* (15 vols., Albany, N. Y., 1853–87), XV, 84.

2. Alexander Hamilton to the Provisional Congress of New York, May
26, July 26, and August, 1776 in Henry Cabot Lodge, ed., *The Works of
Alexander Hamilton* (9 vols.; New York, 1886), VII, 473–76; hereafter
cited as *Lodge*. For the few biographical data included in this book see the
Alexander Hamilton Collection in the Manuscripts Division of the Library
of Congress. See also any of the less biased biographies or those where preju-
dice at least stems from family relationship rather than political attitudes,
such as John Church Hamilton, *The Life of Alexander Hamilton* (2 vols.,
New York, 1840) and *Life of Alexander Hamilton, A History of the Republic of the United States of America as Traced in His Writings and in Those
of His Contemporaries* (4th ed., 7 vols., Boston, 1879); Allen McLane Ham-

Such a task needed to be performed quickly. The Revolution had entered a serious phase, and General Howe's next step was anticipated with foreboding by the leaders of the patriots. However, making well-trained gunners out of undisciplined, enthusiastic volunteers was difficult and time-consuming work. And Hamilton was then only twenty-one years of age.[3]

Yet, with all his work and worries, Hamilton found time not only to fulfill his military duties successfully but also to continue by his own efforts the studies which had been interrupted at King's College. He read a number of significant books and encyclopedias and kept careful notes on most of them. Thus, in the empty space of his Company's Pay Book, he kept about 112 pages of notes, which probably constitute part of a greater body of notes, most of which are perhaps lost.[4]

ilton, *The Intimate Life of Alexander Hamilton* (New York, 1810). Among recent publications the most reliable are Richard B. Morris, *Alexander Hamilton and the Founding of the Nation* (New York, 1957), Broadus Mitchell, *Alexander Hamilton: Youth to Maturity, 1755–1788* (New York, 1957); John C. Miller, *Alexander Hamilton, Portrait in Paradox* (New York, 1959); and Harold C. Syrett and Jean G. Cook, eds., *Interview in Weehawken, The Burr-Hamilton Duel*, with an Introduction and Conclusion by Willard M. Wallace (Middletown, Connecticut, 1960), a collection of documents illuminating an important period of Hamilton's life.

3. Until the appearance of Harold Larson's "Alexander Hamilton: The Fact and Fiction of His Early Years," *William and Mary Quarterly*, 3d Ser., IX (1952), 139–51, the year 1757 had been conventionally accepted as Hamilton's birth date. Since no official records of his birth have been found, the controversy around his age had been settled, in a manner, on the basis of Hamilton's own statement in Alexander Hamilton to Alexander Hamilton [in Scotland], Albany, N. Y., May 2, 1797, in *Lodge*, VIII, 463. There Hamilton implies the year 1757 or 1756 as his birth date. After Larson's documentary evidence, however, it seems proper to correct Hamilton's year of birth from 1757 to 1755. See also *William and Mary Quarterly*, 3d Ser., XII (1955), 330–32.

4. Clear internal evidence of the precise period when Hamilton made these notes is lacking. The uniformity of ink and calligraphy throughout the document suggests that the notes were written continuously during a short period. Differences, if any, between entries on the Company's financial mat-

The existence of this "Pay Book" has been known to scholars since 1850, when John Church Hamilton published the works of his father and, in two pages, gave a "specimen"—and a poor one indeed—of the Notes.[5] Since then, several authors have mentioned or used these two pages, but very few have had the curiosity to examine the manuscript itself, and perhaps no one has ever attempted to make an analytical study of the entire body of the Notes. The fact that they could not be classified as belonging to the principal writings of Hamilton, that they were the work of a young man, and that they looked like school exercises made such material quite unattractive to the students of Hamilton's life. Close examination, however, shows how richly they deserve annotated study. They not only reveal how early Hamilton developed his interest in economics and statesmanship but also shed light on his scholastic background. More important, perhaps, they disclose ideas that recur years later in several of his important papers. Here, concealed in the official garb of military accounts, is a long-neglected source for the thinking of a young man during his formative years.

The "Pay Book" itself[6] is not impressive, the size being 7½ x 6¼ inches. The covering title page, written in flowery eighteenth-century calligraphy by Hamilton himself, reads as follows: "New York, August 31, 1776. Pay Book of the State Company of Artil-

ters and the notes from readings are very small. One should not entirely exclude, however, the possibility that the notes may have been a little later, after 1776 and before 1779; for in the fall of 1779, Hamilton wrote his well-known letter on the National Bank, in which he seems to have used these notes (see below). A chemical analysis of the ink of a document approximately 180 years old offers, unfortunately, wide margin of error and fails to date it exactly. If one excludes, however, the year 1776, which appears on the Pay Book, then a possible date might be the year 1779, when Hamilton's military duties at Morristown allowed him more leisure for reading.

5. John C. Hamilton, ed., *The Works of Alexander Hamilton* (7 vols., New York, 1850), I, 4–5; hereafter cited as *Works* (J. C. Hamilton).

6. Now among the Mss. of the Alexander Hamilton Collection in the Manuscripts Division of the Library of Congress.

lery Commanded by Alex^r Hamilton." The first part contains various accounts of the Artillery Company, and the actual notes appear in the back part.

From the point of view of the material included, these notes can be clearly classified into five categories: first, those involving the economic analysis of several countries; second, those on various other economic subjects; third, those on "political arithmetic," concerning problems of population related to those of government; fourth, extracts from classical authors; and fifth, jottings on miscellaneous subjects.

In the first category, there are notes on a wide range of countries and geographic areas covering most of the world.[7] In analyzing them, one observes that a certain pattern has been applied to almost all the regions. Usually, after a brief statement about the geographic location and size of the country, the following topics are explained: natural resources and products, principal cities and their economic significance, trade and commercial relations of the country. Often discussed are the country's policies on commerce and manufactures and the rate of exchange between local and foreign currency. Although certain of these topics occasionally are omitted, the pattern as a whole remains unchanged.

The notes in this first category, though very enlightening in general, were designed to meet an individual's needs rather than to offer information to an average reader. The uniformity of content and expression, moreover, shows them all to be from the same source, and its identification is not difficult. The kind of information, the style, and the mention of Postelthwayt's name, all reveal that Hamilton's source was *The Universal Dictionary of*

7. The following countries and areas appear under separate headings: America, Asia, Asia Minor, Asia Minor Islands, Austria, Austrian Netherlands, Azores Islands, Bohemia, Britain, British America, Canary Islands, China, Egypt, Europe, Florence, France, Modern Greece, Hungary, Ireland, Netherlands, Portugal, Russia, St. Domingo, Scotland, Spain, Spanish America, Venice.

Trade and Commerce, edited by Malachy Postlethwayt.[8] Indeed, this is almost the sole source of all notes included in the first three categories mentioned above. Ideas and data from other authors, quoted by Hamilton usually by last name only, are all taken from the same work.

It is unfortunate that little if any research has yet been made on the influence of Malachy Postlethwayt on the economic thought of American statesmen during the last quarter of the eighteenth century. His *Universal Dictionary* was an important and almost standard authority for study by responsible public-spirited figures. In its two volumes, statesmen could find an extensive analysis of the economic structure, financial policies, and commercial relations of the most important countries of the world; they could increase their erudition by reading the detailed historical background offered on almost every subject in it, the provisions of many treaties relating to economic questions, and extensive quotations from and references to significant contemporary or classical works. There they could study such topics as public debts, taxes, funds, money, and banks; and they could obtain information on problems relating to the trading companies, colonies, plantations, and many similar themes. Where else could they get so clear a picture of such various situations and derive such ready support for their arguments as from Postlethwayt's abundance of statistical data, tables, charts, and excellent maps? In short, this treasury of information on technical aspects of trade, agriculture, manufacture, and finance could offer more than mere competence. It is of little significance that Postlethwayt was a master of plagiarism and that he often used material from important contemporary authorities without the customary acknowledgement. His statements were an epitome of mid-eighteenth-

8. *The Universal Dictionary of Trade and Commerce, Translated from the French of Monsieur Savary, with Large Additions and Improvements,* by Malachy Postlethwayt (2 vols., 1751–55); hereafter cited as *Postlethwayt.*

century economic theory, and his remarks which followed almost every article, are vivid and convincing.[9]

One can safely say that Postlethwayt's *Dictionary* constitutes the most important document yet discovered showing background and immediate sources of some of Hamilton's principal writings, especially his Reports. Several authors, analyzing his economic thought, have overlooked this work and have struggled with all sorts of hypotheses, endeavoring to explain factors that may have influenced him. Had they consulted the *Dictionary*, they would have found that in most of Hamilton's Reports there are traces of Postlethwayt's economic theories and, indeed, whole paragraphs directly quoted from the *Dictionary*, sometimes masterfully adapted to current American situations.[10]

9. For Postlethwayt (1707?–1767), his economic writings, plagiarisms, and standing in scholarship see Luigi Cossa, *An Introduction to the Study of Political Economy* (London, 1893), p. 252; William Cunningham, *The Growth of English Industry and Commerce in Modern Times* (Cambridge, 1892), pp. 420–21; John Ramsay McCulloch, *A Dictionary, Practical, Theoretical, and Historical of Commerce and Navigation* (London, 1849), p. xxii; William A. S. Hewins, "Malachy Postlethwayt" in *The Dictionary of National Biography*, XVI, 205–06.

10. Among the studies of Hamilton's theoretical background made by serious scholars of an older generation the most significant are perhaps the following: Edward G. Bourne, "Alexander Hamilton and Adam Smith," *Quarterly Journal of Economics*, VIII (328–44, 1894); Charles Franklin Dunbar, "Some Precedents followed by Alexander Hamilton," *ibid.*, III (32–59, 1888), also in his *Economic Essays* (New York, 1904), pp. 71–93; Edward C. Lunt, "Hamilton as a Political Economist," *Journal of Political Economy*, III (289–310, 1895); Jonathan Elliot, "The Funding System of the United States and of Great Britain," *Executive Documents*, II, Doc. No. 15, 28th Cong., 1st Sess. (Washington, 1845). In these essays, however, as well as in the works of William Graham Sumner, Postlethwayt and the *Dictionary* are not mentioned at all. The explanation is probably that these scholars endeavored to locate original sources consulted by Hamilton and not a dictionary such as Postlethwayt's. Twentieth-century scholars, unfortunately, have added almost nothing to the identification of Hamilton's sources, in his writings generally and in his Reports.

Hamilton started using the *Dictionary* quite early. In "The Farmer Refuted," published on February 5, 1775—a year and a half before his note taking in the "Pay Book"—he quoted Postlethwayt twice,[11] mentioning only his name, without giving an exact reference. Both quotations, however, were taken from the *Dictionary*.[12] In subsequent articles, he borrowed frequently and heavily from the *Dictionary*, but he never again acknowledged the source of his information. Consciously or not, he treated Postlethwayt in the same manner as the latter had previously treated most of the authors he had used.

In his notes in the "Pay Book," following the same policy, Hamilton never mentioned the entries he had used or even the title of the *Dictionary*. Nevertheless, copying Postlethwayt's exact wording and often combining material from two or more of the articles, he used, in all, excerpts from thirty-eight of its entries.[13]

In his notes in the second category, Hamilton examined the following economic topics: funds, money, circulation of money, money coined in England, coin, labor, landed interest, and the Dutch fisheries. In addition, attracted perhaps by their curious composition, he kept detailed notes on glass and amianthus. There is, also, a note on "a short rule to determine the interest." These notes do not cover all the aspects of the subjects under examination, but only those phases in which Hamilton himself was interested. Already evident, however, is the nature of the topics that attracted his attention, topics destined to dominate his activities and thoughts for the rest of his life. All of those notes, with the exception of the last one, on interest, were copied word for word from various entries in the *Dictionary*. Even when Hamilton gave an extensive definition of money and added as a refer-

11. *Lodge*, I, 137–38, 141.
12. *Postlethwayt*, I, 532–33, 536: entry "Colonies."
13. Except for Asia Minor, Ireland, St. Domingo, Scotland, most of these appear in footnote 7; the others are Amianthus, Anatolia, Annuities, Asbestos, Circulation, Coin, Exchange, Fisheries, Funds, Glass, Gold, Labour, Landed Interest, Money, People.

ence "Aristotle's *Politics*, Chapter 6,"[14] or when he quoted Sir Isaac Newton on the parity between gold and silver, he took the exact text and references from the *Dictionary*, in the first case from the entry "Money" and in the second from the entry "Coin."

The third category of Hamilton's notes deals with political arithmetic, a subject very close to his heart. Included are tables and statistical data on the synthesis of population and the ratio between births and deaths.

It was just prior to the seventeenth century that people, amazed at the progress of mathematics, developed a faith in this science and endeavored to explain almost everything in mathematical terms. Shortly thereafter, Newton's great contributions strengthened this faith, and soon a new field developed applying mathematics to subjects relating to social problems and government. Sir William Petty's *Political Arithmetic* gave the name to this field,[15] and it came to be regarded as the duty of all statesmen to be versed in the mathematics of political science. Hamilton very early realized the significance of this new branch of mathematics, and political arithmetic became the foundation of his calculations on public affairs in later years, for it was evident that no clear picture could be obtained of the wealth, production and consumption, revenues, movements in trade, agriculture and manufactures, or even of the military strength of the country, without a competent knowledge of the flunctuations and composition of the population and the relation between births and deaths. When Hamilton called Postlethwayt "the ablest master of politi-

14. *Postlethwayt*, II, 282; I, 528.

15. Sir William Petty (1623–1687) first published a small book on this subject together with a Captain John Graunt, *Natural and Political Observations . . . Made upon the Bills of Mortality* [of the city of London] (London, 1662); this was followed by two similar studies in 1682 and 1683; three years later he published his *Two Essays in Political Arithmetic* (London, 1686); and in the year of his death he published his *Five Essays in Political Arithmetic* (London, 1687).

cal arithmetic,"[16] he certainly extended to him one of his greatest compliments.

In the notes of this category, Hamilton quoted data and tables composed by several authors, but he gave most of the space to Dr. Edmond Halley's tables on the mortality of mankind, especially to his statistics on the duration of life of the population of Breslau, Silesia.

In the fourth category are fifty-one pages of notes all taken from Plutarch, with the exception of one from Demosthenes. Explaining why he kept them, Hamilton stated: "These notes are selected more for their singularity than use—though some important facts are comprehended."[17] There are, indeed, several "important facts" in the material, and it is not surprising that Hamilton sought for them in Plutarch. As Morison has very pertinently observed concerning the early American statesmen: "These men were *not* fitted for public responsibility by courses in civics, sociology and psychology, but by the study of Plutarch's *Lives,* of the orations of Cicero and Demosthenes and of Thucydides."[18] There Hamilton could find fine examples of statesmanship, lofty political ethos, and remarkable precedents; and there he could enrich his knowledge with the experience of the political failures and successes of the ancients.

Up to the time of his military career, the main body of his education was classical. Though his first training in St. Croix was limited, perhaps, to the three R's, it is very probable that his

16. "The Continentalist," No. VI (July 4, 1782) in *Lodge,* I, 267. Though, as usual, no reference is given by Hamilton, the statement quoted by him was taken from *Postlethwayt,* II, 13, entry "Landed Interest," which is identical with *Postlethwayt,* I, 879, and 880, entry "Funds."

17. On the significance of Plutarch as a source illuminating Hamilton's views on politics and his personal ambitions, see Douglass Adair, "A Note on Certain of Hamilton's Pseudonyms," *William and Mary Quarterly,* 3rd Ser., XII (1955), 282–97. Adair, however, made no use of material from the "Pay Book."

18. Samuel Eliot Morison, *The Ancient Classics in a Modern Democracy* (London, 1939), p. 23.

teacher, Dr. Hugh Knox, a Princeton graduate, initiated him into the world of the classics. Later, in 1773, he spent a year in the grammar school of Francis Barber at Elizabethtown, New Jersey, preparing himself for his entrance to college. His curriculum there is quite obscure, but the entrance requirements of both Princeton, which he planned to attend, and King's College, which he finally entered, are known. Hamilton had to prepare himself in order to meet them, and both colleges included in their requirements a knowledge of Virgil, Cicero's Orations, and Latin grammar; Princeton, moreover, required that the candidate should be "so well acquainted with the Greek as to render any part of the four Evangelists in that language into Latin or English; and to give the grammatical connection of the words. . . ."[19]

When Hamilton entered King's College, he found one of the most complete classical curricula offered in America during the second half of the eighteenth century. In this comparatively young college, the first three years were devoted to the study of classics.[20] Among the authors studied were Virgil, Ovid, Aesop, Lucian, Cicero, Epictetus, Pliny, Horace, Aristotle, Plato, Xenophon, Theocritus, Tacitus, Sophocles, Euripides, Aeschylus, Thucydides, Dionysius of Halicarnassus, and Isocrates; in addition, there was training in Latin and Greek grammar and rhetoric.[21] Hamilton, because of a special agreement with the college and the two years' time he studied there, perhaps did not carry all this classical load. Thus, it was quite natural that Hamilton de-

19. For the entrance requirements at Princeton see John Maclean, *History of the College of New Jersey* (Philadelphia, 1877), I, 132; at King's College, *A History of Columbia University, 1754–1904* (New York, 1904), app. B, p. 446.

20. *Minutes of the Governors of the College of the Province of New York in America, 1755–1768, and of the Corporation of King's College in the City of New York, 1768–1770*, Minutes of March 1, 1763 (New York, 1932). This curriculum remained almost unchanged until Hamilton's time.

21. *Ibid.*

voted almost half of his "Pay Book" notes to the writings of ancient Greece and Rome.

Hamilton quotes four of Plutarch's *Lives:* Theseus, Romulus, Lycurgus, and Numa Pompilius. Most of the time the notes constitute free outlines of Plutarch's statements, and since they were probably taken in a rather free style for private use, they include several mistakes in spelling and punctuation. They contain a certain amount of mythology, a number of those charming stories that make reading Plutarch so attractive, and much description of Athenian, Spartan, and Roman life. There are two subjects, however, to which Hamilton devoted the greater part of this group of notes.

The first, as might be expected, concerned the governmental practices and political institutions of antiquity. Thus one reads notes on the early social stratification of the Athenians; the distinction by the Romans between patricians and the "populace," the relationship between patrons and clients, and the division of the Romans into tribes and curiae; the institution of the helots in Sparta and the practice of the cryptiae; the establishment of the Roman Senate and the Spartan Gerousia; the Spartan kings; the inclination of Theseus toward popular government; and the absolutism of Romulus. One finds condensations of material on the Spartan Ephori, the power of the early Athenian magistrates to interpret and administer the law, and the legislative power in Sparta. There are summaries of many articles: Numa's land reform and his encouragement to agriculture; Lycurgus' redistribution of land, division, of property, and coinage system; the reaction of the rich Lacedaemonians against Lycurgus' reforms; and various other subjects such as the institution of the Roman Pontifices, the synthesis of the Roman legions, the mode of Spartan elections, and the civic duties of the Lacedaemonians.

The second subject on which Hamilton kept extensive notes is probably interesting to those who attempt a Freudian analysis of his complex personality. It deals with love themes in legends and stories or in habits and customs which found expression in a more or less irregular way.

Thus one reads of the passionate love of Theseus' wife, Phaedra, for her son Hippolytus; how King Tharsetius offered his daughter as a mistress to the god Priapus, how she replaced herself with her servant, and how the fruit of this relation was the birth of Romulus and Remus; the whipping of young married women by two naked young noblemen during the celebration of the Lupercalia in Rome and "how the young married women were glad of this kind of whipping as they imagined it helped conception"; and the relations between young Spartan men and women and the festivities where "the virgins should go naked as well as the young men and in this manner dance in their presence." Included are exerpts on the promotion of marriage in Sparta, the quasi-forcible abduction of brides, and subsequent marital habits; how old husbands in Sparta loaned their young wives to young men and thus acquired worthy children; the concept of adultery in Sparta; the institution of lovers for every lad; the love of a certain mountain nymph for Numa and the frequent meetings of the two in private; and the relations of Hercules with his mistress Larentia. Perhaps Hamilton had in mind these notes when he stated at the beginning that they "are selected more for their singularity."

Besides the material from Plutarch, Hamilton included in the notes two quotations from Demosthenes' *Orations*.

The fifth, and last, category includes a few of Hamilton's memoranda and random thoughts. There is, for instance, a long list of articles which he probably planned to study from Postlethwayt's *Dictionary*.

John C. Hamilton in his edition of the *Works* of his father, gives a list of twenty-eight books[22] which he says is contained in

___

22. *Works* (J. C. Hamilton), I, 4. The following is the list of these books as they appear, with frequent erroneous spelling: "Rousseau's Emilius; Smith's History of New York; Leonidas; View of the Universe; Lex Merca-

the manuscript of the "Pay Book." It is not clear if Hamilton had bought or used or intended to obtain the books in the list, which covered a variety of titles from Rousseau's *Emile* to Ralph Cudworth's *The True Intellectual System of the Universe*. In the "Pay Book" notes, none of these books has been quoted, with the exception of Demosthenes' *Orations*. Since this list of books is not included in the extant manuscript of the "Pay Book," it seems evident that it must have been derived from one of the now missing pages. After Alexander Hamilton's death, at least ten books from this list were found in his library.[23]

One interesting item of both lists is the misspelled "Ralt's *Dictionary of Trade and Commerce*." This is Richard Rolt's *A New Dictionary of Trade and Commerce*, published in London in 1756 (hereafter referred to as *Rolt*). In a subtitle, Rolt added: "Compiled from the information of the most Eminent Merchants and from the works of the best writers on Commercial Subjects in all Languages." What he did not make clear was the fact that he had copied whole parts from Postlethwayt's *Dictionary*, often using the same wording. Despite this plagiarism, Rolt offered a

toria; Milhot's History of France; Memoirs of the House of Brandeburgh. Review of the characters of the principal Nations of Europe; Review of Europe; History of Prussia; History of France; Lasset's Voyage through Italy; Robinson's Charles V; Present State of Europe; Grecian History; Baretti's Travels; Bacon's Essays; Philosophical Transactions; Hobbe's Dialogues; Plutarch's Morals; Cicero's Morals; Orations Demosthenes; Cudworth's Intellectual System; Entick's History of the Late War; European settlements in America; Ralt's Dictionary of Trade and Commerce; Winn's History of America; Montaigne's Essays."

23. These books are the following, listed by Allan McLane Hamilton, *The Intimate Life of Alexander Hamilton,* 74–75, with spelling almost identical to that appearing in John C. Hamilton's list: "Robertson's Charles V; Bacon's Essays; Hobbe's Dialogues; Cicero's Morals; Orations, Demosthenes; Cudworth's Intellectual system; Enticle's History of the Late War; Ralt's Dictionary of Trade and Commerce; Winn's History of America; Montaign's Essays." The complete list of books in Hamilton's library appears in *Works* (J. C. Hamilton).

new kind of dictionary on commerce: it was concise, clear, relieved of theoretic disputations; it was closer to what a practical businessman needed. There is a great possibility that Hamilton used it. Therefore, whenever in the text there is an identical wording in the two dictionaries, or where it was deemed expedient to mention Rolt's version, there is a brief reference to it.

Among these miscellaneous notes, there is one expressing dissatisfaction with the American diplomatic representatives abroad and the members of Congress who were not well informed on international affairs. Hamilton asked: "What intelligence has been given to Congress by our ministers of the designs, strength by sea & land, actual interests & views of the different powers in Europe?" A similar idea, perhaps, had induced him to collect all the information on foreign countries which he included in the Pay Book. In the same section he also expressed his opinion that the tax collectors should be appointed by Congress rather than by the states.

It is not certain to what extent Hamilton later used his notes. The economic analysis of foreign countries, though offering a great deal of information, could not have helped him very much. The compilation of facts was originally made by Postlethwayt before 1750. Within the next thirty or forty years, important changes were to take place on the international scene, and Hamilton later could refer to situations described in his notes as history. The major part of the rest contributed to building a broad background rather than to helping in the solution of specific problems. Nevertheless, the study of Hamilton's works reveals that years later and during his most creative period, he went back to his "Pay Book" and incorporated in major writings some of the information found there.

Thus, in his "First Report on the Public Credit,"[24] communicated to the House of Representatives on January 14, 1790, Hamilton drew from his old notes on political arithmetic. In this Re-

24. *American State Papers, Finance,* I. 32.

port, which constitutes one of his most important papers, Hamilton, in computing the annuities which would be enjoyed by certain persons in certain cases, used a whole page from his "Pay Book" notes. The notes were originally taken from the *Dictionary* entry "Annuities" and include Dr. Edmond Halley's tables on the duration of life.[25]

In his "Report on the Establishment of a Mint,"[26] communicated to the House of Representatives on January 28, 1791, writing about the desirable ratio between gold and silver, he quoted his note, which included Newton's proposition as well as Postlethwayt's statement, that the ratio of the two metals throughout Europe was 1 to 15.[27] Hamilton, however, was somewhat cautious because of the time that had elapsed since Newton made his calculations and hence added the following reservation:

> But however accurate and decisive this authority may be deemed, in relation to the period to which it applies, it cannot be taken, at the distance of more than seventy years, as a rule for determining the existing proportion. Alterations have been since made in the regulations of their coins, by several nations which as well as the course of trade, have an influence upon the market values. Nevertheless; there is reason to believe that the state of the matter, as represented by Sir Isaac Newton, is not very remote from its actual state.[28]

In his "Report on Manufactures,"[29] communicated to the House of Representatives on December 5, 1791, Hamilton copied almost word for word the entire page on glass from his "Pay

25. On the use of Halley's tables and Hamilton's silence on Dr. Richard Price's more up-to-date and popular calculations, see C. F. Dunbar, *Economic Essays*, p. 83, fn. 2.

26. *American State Papers, Finance,* I, 94.

27. Hamilton took his quotation of Newton's proposition from *Postlethwayt*, I, 528, entry "Coin" and Postlethwayt's statement from *ibid.*, II, 282, entry "Money."

28. *American State Papers, Finance,* I, 94. Postlethwayt's data are given in *ibid.*, 92–94.

29. *Ibid.*, 143.

Book,"[30] which in turn had been copied from the entry "Glass" of the *Dictionary*.

The use of the material contained in the notes is widespread and diverse, oftentimes adapted for a particular purpose. In one of his notes on France one reads:

Lewis the 14th in June 1700 established the Council of Commerce consisting of some of the principal officers of State and twelve merchants chosen and paid by the principal trading towns, to represent all things relative to trade and manufactures and propose regulations etc.—infinite good has resulted to France from this institution. The salaries are about 400 S Stg per annum.[31]

While still in the army, Hamilton, being deeply concerned with the financial stability of the country, proposed in a letter to a member of Congress a plan for the establishment of a national bank; in this amazing document, among other suggestions, he advised as follows:

XII. The bank to be managed by the trustees of the company, under the inspection of the Board of Trade* (*This board ought immediately to be established at all events. The Royal Council of Commerce, in France, and the subordinate chambers in each province, form an excellent institution, and may, in many respects, serve as a model. . . .)[32]

30. While in this and other cases there is no doubt that Hamilton did go back to his notes in the "Pay Book," there are several instances in his Reports, where he used material not included in the notes but which he took from *Postlethwayt's Dictionary*. It seems that either this additional material was contained in pages of the "Pay Book" now lost or, and this is very probable, Hamilton performed a more scholarly and careful work by resorting again to the *Dictionary*. The material on "Glass" is identical in the "Pay Book" and in the *Dictionary* so that the immediate source here is indeterminable.

31. Taken from *Postlethwayt*, I, 832, entry "France."

32. *Lodge*, III, 76. While the letter does not indicate the addressee, Lodge maintains that it was sent to Robert Morris; he dates it in 1779 in one place (I, xv), and in 1780 in another (III, 61). Nathan Schachner, *Alexander Hamilton* (New York, 1946), 97–98, on the other hand, asserts

In another instance, in "The Continentalist," No. VI, (July 4, 1782),[33] Hamilton used his notes on the value of the production and consumption of Great Britain and on the proportion between her exports and imports.[34]

Another interesting example of adaptation appears in a letter of 1781 to Robert Morris, in which Hamilton, taking into consideration the factor of immigration and relying on his favorite subject of political arithmetic, changed Postlethwayt's ratio of population increase as it was quoted in his notes.[35] In this communication, again on the topic of the National Bank, he asserted:

> Our population will be doubled in thirty years; there will be a confluence of emigrants from all parts of the world, our commerce will have a proportionable progress, and of course our wealth and capacity for revenue.[36]

Using the same statistics seven years later when he spoke before the New York State Convention for the ratification of the Constitution, Hamilton foresaw the following increase: "At present we have three millions of people; in twenty-five years we shall have six millions; and in forty years nine millions."[37]

Although it seem that Hamilton took notes on Plutarch's writings more for "their singularity" than for use, he had this author in mind on several occasions when he turned to subjects from ancient Greece and Rome; for instance, he made a direct reference to the life of Pericles in the "Federalist," No. VI. The ex-

that the recipient of this letter was General John Sullivan and that the letter was written in Nov. 1779. The latter's opinion is shared by most scholars. See also Joseph Charles, "Hamilton and Washington: The Origins of the American Party System," *William and Mary Quarterly*, 3d Ser., XII, 1955, 242.

33. *Lodge*, I, 267.
34. Taken from *Postlethwayt*, I, 879, entry "Funds."
35. Taken from *Postlethwayt*, II, 438, entry "People."
36. Hamilton to Morris, Apr. 30, 1781, *Lodge*, III, 124.
37. Jonathan Elliot, ed., *The Debates in the Several State Conventions on the Adoption of the Federal Constitution* (Philadelphia, 1836), II, 252.

amples, however, were not taken from the four *Lives* he included in his "Pay Book" notes.

Nevertheless, it would be wrong to suppose that Hamilton did not use these notes at all. In a few cases, he remembered them in a much later period. These cases, however, are very few considering the great number of Hamilton's notes on Plutarch.

Hamilton's interests developed at an early age and, as expressed in his "Pay Book" notes, remained with him during the rest of his life. An illuminating example is the following question he asked in one of his notes. It implies a strong nationalistic feeling which, as far as is known, he expresses here for the first time:

> Quere? Would it be advisable to let all taxes even those imposed by the States be collected by persons of Congressional appointment and would it not be advisable to pay the collectors so much per cent on the sums collected?

A few years later, on July 4, 1782, he came back to the same question, publicly this time, explaining that:

> The reason of allowing Congress to appoint its own officers of the customs, collectors of the taxes, and military officers of every rank, is to create in the interior of each state a mass of influence in favor of the Federal Government.[38]

On January 27, 1783, in a speech in Congress, he strongly opposed the idea that the states should appoint the collectors of revenue for the use of the government, characterizing it as "a system by which the collectors were chosen by the people, and made their offices more subservient to their popularity than to

38. "The Continentalist," *Lodge,* I, 272. It was the same thought that induced Hamilton a year earlier, on April 30, 1781, in a letter to Robert Morris, to make the frequently-quoted statement that "a national debt, if it is not excessive, will be to us a national blessing. It will be a powerful cement of the Union."—*Lodge,* III, 124. Nine years later, in his "First Report on the Public Credit," he maintained again that "the proper funding of the present debt will render it a national blessing."—*American State Papers, Finance,* I, 24.

the public revenue." He advocated their appointment by Congress "as being more economical, since the collection would be effected with fewer officers under the management of Congress than under that of the States."[39] The next day, Hamilton returned to his proposal, revealing his whole purpose:

> Mr. Hamilton, in reply to Mr. Ellsworth, dwelt long on the inefficacy of State funds. . . . As an additional reason for the latter to be collected by officers under appointment of Congress, he signed that as the energy of the Federal Government was evidently short of the degree necessary for pervading and uniting the States, it was expedient to introduce the influence of officers deriving their emoluments from, and consequently interested in supporting the power of Congress.[40]

He was so thoroughly convinced of the expediency of his plan that he did not realize the political blunder he was making, because this very increase of federal authority was the main fear of his opponents. Madison, recording this incident, described it as "imprudent and injurious to the cause it was meant to serve." Madison noted that Hamilton's opponents "smiled at the disclosure" and that "Mr. Bland, and still more Mr. Lee, who were of this number, took notice in private conversation that Mr. Hamilton had let out the secret."[41]

A month later, on February 12, 1783, Hamilton offered in Congress the following Resolution:

> *Resolved*, that it is the opinion of Congress that complete JUSTICE cannot be done to the creditors of the United States, nor restoration of PUBLIC CREDIT be effected, nor the future exigencies of the war provided for, but by the establishment of permanent and adequate funds to operate generally throughout the United States, *to be collected by Congress*.[42]

39. Elliot, *Debates*, V, 33.

40. *Ibid.*, V, 35.

41. Irving Brant, *James Madison* (3 vols., New York, 1948), II, 227-28. See also Gaillard Hunt, ed., *The Writings of James Madison* (New York, 1900), I, 336.

42. *Lodge*, I, 285; the emphasis is Hamilton's.

On May 14, of the same year, explaining to Governor Clinton why, among other reasons, he considered a proposed plan of funding the public debt as inadequate and had voted against it in Congress, he stated that:

> . . . the nomination and appointment of the collectors of the revenue are to reside in the State [according to the proposed plan] instead of at least the nomination being in the United States; the consequence of which will be that those states which have little interest in the funds, by having a small share of the public debt due to their own citizens, will take care to appoint such persons as are least likely to collect the revenue.[43]

One can imagine Hamilton's satisfaction when on November 1, 1791, he saw the materialization of his idea, fifteen years after he first expressed it. On that date, George Washington communicated to Congress a report announcing the arrangement made by the President of the United States with respect to the revenue districts, the appointment of the tax collectors, the assignment of their compensation, etc. This report merely echoed the "Report on Spirits, Foreign and Domestic," framed by Hamilton and signed by him, as Secretary of the Treasury, the day before. Hamilton's Report embodied the second part of his original note in the "Pay Book," namely, that it would be advisable to pay the revenue collectors "so much per cent on the sums collected."[44] Hamilton had strongly emphasized the significance of such a provision in the previous year when, in his report to the House of Representatives of April 23, 1790, on "Operations of the Act Laying Duties on Imports," he stressed that the security of the revenue greatly depended on such a measure and that it was "certain that competent allowances are essential to the idea of having the service performed by characters worthy of trust."[45] Even after the establishment of this principle by law, Hamilton

---

43. Hamilton to Clinton, May 14, 1783, *Lodge,* VIII, 117.
44. *American State Papers, Finance,* I, 110-11.
45. *Ibid.,* 48.

returned to the subject again on March 6, 1792. In another "Report on Spirits, Foreign and Domestic," communicated to the House of Representatives on March 6, 1792, he asked for an increase of the rewards given for the "diligent services of respectable and trustworthy" collectors, as "essential to the execution of the law in a manner effectual to the purposes of the Government and satisfactory to the community."[46]

The notes included in the "Pay Book of the State Company of Artillery" undoubtedly enlighten several aspects of his career, help to follow the unfolding and development of some of his ideas, and contribute to a better understanding of his significant personality.

46. *Ibid.,* 158.

II

The Pay Book with Hamilton's Notes

The Continent of Europe is 2600 miles long and 2800 miles broad.

o   o   o   o   o

96**

The Dutch in the Greenland fishery have from 150 to 200 sail and ten thousand seamen.

It is ordered that in their public prayers they pray that it would please God to bless the governments the Lords the States and their great and small fisheries.[1]

---

* Hamilton's page numbering.

† A difference in handwriting in most of this numbering system, and the letter "p" preceding some entries, as well as the use of darker ink, indicates this paging was the work of another hand, which numbered only the recto pages and left the verso unnumbered.

1. *Postlethwayt*, I, 783, entry "Fisheries." Postlethwayt's statement is related to the prayers is as follows: "This branch of trade is of such unspeakable concern to the Dutch, that, in their public prayers, it is appointed to be mentioned, when they pray to the Supreme Being, THAT IT WOULD PLEASE HIM TO BLESS THE GOVERNMENT, THE LORDS, THE STATES, AND ALSO THEIR GREAT AND SMALL FISHERIES."

The Dutch were computed by Sir Walter Raleigh to have 3000 ships and fifty thousand seamen employed in the herring fishery 9000 more ships and 150,000 seamen more in exporting and vending. The province of Holland in the whole having 20,000 ships.[2]

o o o o o

96**   p. 228

Glass is a compound of sand or stone and vegetable salts— 100 pounds of sand will produce 150 pounds of glass — The kind of sand or stone is of that species called tarso — the white chrystalline‡ and flinty—The salt is produced from a sea weed called kali, or for want of this from wormwood, woad, alga, common thistle, bramble, hops and the whole leguminous tribe.

The proportion for crystal glass is 200 pounds of tarso to 130 of salt.

These are put into an oven or reverberatory furnace and calcined for five hours when it becomes frit.

The frit is put into melting pots with a kind of blackish stone called Manganese to render it more clear and azure.[3]

o o o o o

2. Sir Walter Raleigh is quoted by De Witt, who in turn is quoted in *Postlethwayt*, I, 783-84, entry "Fisheries." It is from here that Hamilton took his note. Rolt also quotes both Sir Walter Raleigh and De Witt and offers a great deal of similar information in the entry "Fishery."

  ** Hamilton followed customary bookkeeping practice, using the same number on verso and recto pages. Hamilton's paging ends here.

  ‡ Hamilton's spelling, punctuation, etc., are reproduced without editing.

3. *Postlethwayt*, I, 896–97, entry "Glass." In his "Report on Manufactures," communicated to the House of Representatives on December 5, 1791, Hamilton, referring to the production of glass in this country, stated "The materials for making glass are found everywhere. In the United States there is no deficiency of them. The sands and stones called *tarso* which include flinty and crystalline substances generally, and the salts of various plants, particularly of the sea-weed kali, or kelp, constitute the essential ingredients. An extraordinary abundance of fuel is a particular advantage enjoyed by this country for such manufactures. They, however, require large capitals, and involve much manual labor. . . ." *Lodge,* IV, 189. In writing

Asia Minor. Pamphylia produces a great number of goats whose hair make excellent camblets.[4]

Greece is a fertile country now divided into Macedonia, Albania, Epirus, Thessaly and Achaia — Macedonia has rich mines of gold.

Achaia produces rice, cotton, tobacco.

Greece in general has plenty of corn wine and oil — several parts produce silk — its wool is coarse and bad.

Salonichi or Thessalonicha is one of the principal cities and best ports in Greece; it has near 300,000 people — Constantinople is near it.[5]

o   o   o   o   o

229

Asia Minor

Smyrna the most considerable town in Asia Minor — has one of the best ports in the Levant and the greatest trade of this part of the Turkish Dominions.

The River Pactolus remarkable for its golden sands runs through Lydia in Asia Minor.

The country about Tocat produces a great variety of excellent plants and particularly some Fossilia or subterraneous vegetations of surprising beauty. They are something like our flints

his Reports, Hamilton on several occasions went back to the notes of the "Pay Book" and copied information found there. Often, he performed a more careful and scholarly work by resorting again to Postlethwayt. In the statements on glass made in his "Report on Manufactures," Hamilton disregarded the wealth of information given by Postlethwayt and he exclusively used the above page of his "Pay Book" notes. These statements, however, constitute a fine example of adaptation of his notes to the American realities.

4. *Postlethwayt,* I, 60, entry "Anatolia." The same information is also offered by Jacques Savary des Bruslons and M. Philemon-Louis Savary in their *Dictionnaire universel de commerce* (Paris, 1748), I, 348, entry "Angouri, autrement Angora & Beibazar." This dictionary (hereafter cited as *Savary*) was Postlethwayt's acknowledged principal source of information.

5. *Postlethwayt,* I, 914–15, entry "Greece."

inclosed in matrices, which when broken display some of the finest chrystallizations that can be imagined.

The High Chain of Mountains in Capadocia called Antitaurus have mines of silver copper iron allum etc. There is a great deal of saffron and fine marble in several parts of Asia Minor.[6]

o o o o o

Postlethwait

Britain

Lies between 50 & 59 d. N L Long from 5 to 600 miles — Greatest breadth 300

Chief productions of England.

	Corn	Cheese	Rock salt	Fuller's earth
thirty⎱	Timber	Hides	Alum	Pipe and
sheet⎰	Cattle	Beer & Malt	Copperas	Potter's clay
	flax	Spirits	Lapis Calaminaris	
	Wool	Cyder	stones of divers sorts	
	Salt	Tin	for building paving etc.	
	Tallow	Copper	Slate	
	Butter	Lead	Oker	
		Iron		

Manufactures
of wool, hair
& cotton
⎱ Cloth of several sorts. Serges, perpets, says,
shalloons. Stuffs of various kinds. Bays
flannels dimities fustians Camblets mohairs
grogams etc. Blankets, rugs carpets —

Manufactures
of silk
⎱ Lace
Velvets
Brocades
Sattins
Taffeties
Damasks
Lustring
Mantuas
Sarsenets

6. *Postlethwayt*, I, 59–60, entry "Anatolia."

o o o o o

Britain

Manufactures
of Flax & Hemp { Linnens of various sorts
Lace
Thread
Cordage
Paper

Manufactures
of Timber { Ships and vessels of all sorts
Casks of all kinds

Manufactures
of Metal
{
Artillery
Cannon mortars
Bullets boms, etc.

Coin and   { Gold
Wrought plate Silver
               Copper

Bells of all sizes   Pipes and Vessels
of mixed metals   for culinary and
Coppers   other domestic
Caldrons   uses of Iron
Furnaces   Brass Copper
Statues of Brass or lead   Pewter lead **silver**
Balustres, or pallisadoes   Gold
  Edged tools   iron)   Silver
  Engines | Wire Copper
  Weapons   brass }   Iron
  Armour of   steele | Brass
    all sorts   )   Steel

o o o o o

27

Britain

Manufactures
of skins
& hair
of beasts

{ Parchment
Vellum
Leather of which are made furs for cloathing
Hats & caps, shoes & boots
Saddles, harness and furniture for horses
Gloves & garments coaches and
chairs. Household stuffs covers
of books etc.

Products and manufactures of Scotland and
Ireland much the same except fir timber
plaiding and striped muslins peculiar to
the former.

The coal trade an immence trade
employs near 1500 sail of shipping and
seamen in proportion besides watermen
lightermen etc. You may see 600 colliers
before the city of London at a time —
Another branch of the coasting
trade Tin from Cornwall, rock salt from
Lancashire — cheese and lead from
Chester — culm from Swanzey in Wales
the whole employs 300 sail. She[7]

o   o   o   o   o

231

These and several other branches of coasting trade for corn
fish cyder glass etc. are computed to employ 100,000 persons.

The Hardware manufactures Birmingham and Sheffield — the
latter employes 40,000 people.

The woolen manufactors employs a million of people — the
consumption at home amounts to a million sterlings *per ann.*

Their fisheries a large branch — consist of herring Pilchards

7. The last line of the manuscript page has been cut off.

mackarel oysters, Lobsters — Salmon taken in the Severn.

Scotland produces grain which it sends partly to Spain Holland Norway — for trees of an immense size — a great number of black cattle — wool which goes chiefly to England.

A fine manufacture of worsted stockings at Aberdeen.

Large linnen manufactures and fine fisheries in Scotland.

o o o o o

Scotland has a fine salt manufacture and exports great quantities annualy to Germany Norway and the Baltic.

Ireland is chiefly a country of grazing though they have also a good deal of corn — they have a great many quarries of free stone slate marble, and sea coal but their principal fuel is turf. They have some glass works the sand for which comes from England.

Their exports consist in cattle hides furs tallow butter cheese honey wax salt hemp linnen-cloth timber pipe staves wool and woolen-cloth coarse rugs and shag mantles freezes ratteens, camblets, salmon herring etc. some lead tin and iron.

The Irish have immense quantities of Excellent Wool — They sheer their sheep twice a year.

o o o o o

232

The Irish from the restraint on their manufactures clandestinely export great quantities of unwrought wool to France.

They trade a great deal with Flanders and the low countries especially for butter tallow and leather.

They carry on a great trade for beef with France.

They have a large herring fishery which they send to Spain and Portugal.

The Ballance of Trade with the Portuguese not so considerable in favour of the English as is imagined.

Trade with Spain declined latterly by the interference with the French no large ballance in favour of England.

The Ballance with Italy against England.

o o o o o

Trade with Turkey rather advantageous in the light of giving rise to new manufactures by the raw silk imported thence.

Among other articles exported to Germany are *tobacco ginger sugar*.

Hamburg and Germany has a ballance against England — they furnish her with large quantities of linnen —

In the trade with Holland a considerable ballance in favour of England.

Trade with France greatly against England.

The trade with Flanders in favour of England.

A large ballance in favour of Norway and Denmark.

Ballance in favour of Sweden.

Great ballance in favour of Russia.

o   o   o   o   o

233

Indian trade very advantageous upon the whole a vast quantity of raw silk brought from thence.[8]

o   o   o   o   o

Rate of Exchange with the several nations in 52.

To Venice for a ducat 51 d. ¾ Par 49. d. 492. Loss 4½ per cent
Leghorn for a dollar — 50 d.º 51.69 Gain 1⅞ per cent
Genoa in favour of England not mentioned
Lisbon for a milree 5/5⅞ Par 67.166 Gain not 2 per cent
Antwerp a stg. for 36.5 Par 35/.17 Gain 3⅞ per cent
Amsterdam d.º for 35.4.2 Par 36/.59 Loss 3½ per cent
Hamburgh d.º for 33.5 Par 35/.17 Loss 5 per cent
Exchanges with Norway Sweden Russia and most parts of Germany are carried on through Amsterdam and Hamburgh at an equal disadvantage.
To Madrid for a piece 8/8 40⅞ Par 43.2 Gain above 6½ per cent

8. This item and the seven preceding pages are from *Postlethwayt*, I, 344–48, 350–51, entry "Britain."

To Paris for the crown⎱
   of three livres   ⎰ 31d ⁷⁄₁₆ Par 29d.149   Loss above 7⅛
   per cent.[9]

o   o   o   o   o

234

Postlethwaite supposes the quantity of cash necessary to carry
on the circulation in a state one third of the rents to the land
proprietors or 1/9 the whole product of the lands.

   — See the articles Cash and Circulation.[10]

o   o   o   o   o

France

Has an immense inland commerce carried on principally by
rivers the chief of which are the Seine, the Loire, the Soan, the
Rhone and the Garonne — There are five rivers empty into the
Seine not far from Paris and near eighty large cities that have a
direct commerce with it by water. Tis supposed to contain near
a million of inhabitants and the villages in the neighborhood half
a million more —

Lyons situated at the confluence of the Soan and Rhosne.
The second city of France is to the Southern provinces what Paris
is to the Northern. It drives an immense inland commerce chiefly
by water communications. By means of the Rhosne it communi-
cates with Geneva and all Switzerland and hence by the River
Aar with the Rhine and several parts of Germany.[11]

o   o   o   o   o

235

By the Durance a large river but rapid it trades through Pied-
mont with Italy and brings home the productions of that country
— It is supposed to contain 200,000 people.

9. The above table was made by Hamilton who combined in this case
data from Sir Isaac Newton's *Tables* and the Lloyd list as of the 21st of
April, 1752 cited in *Postlethwayt*, I, 352–53, entry "Britain."

10. *Postlethwayt*, I, 464, entry "Cash," and 499, entry "Circulation."
Rolt, on the other hand, mentions "Sir William Petty was of opinion, that
the cash, or circulating money in a state, is equal to the tenth part of the
annual product of the land."— *Rolt*, entry "Cash."

11. *Postlethwayt*, I, 808–10, entry "France."

Marseilles on the Mediterranean is one of the principal sea ports of France.

Toulon is the best Harbour of France. It has immense naval Magazines and arsenals a very large foundery for cannon — At the time it was besieged by the confederates in 1707 it had fifty four French ships of the line from first to fourth rates in the harbour —

Lewis the fourteenth was fifteen years with vast labour and expence uniting the Cantabrian [Calabrian] with the Mediterranean Sea by a canal.[12]

The French have a considerable smuggling trade of wool from England by way of Bologne at the entrance of the Soam from whence passing to

o   o   o   o   o

Amiens and Rouen it gives rise to flourishing woolen manufacturers in imitation of those of England —[13]

Marigolante produces cinnamon trees — S Domingo (belonging to F and S) is 400 miles long and 120 broad — 400 leagues in circumference. It is the largest of the Antilles — It has large forests of palms elms oaks pines juniper caramite acajou — great abundance of cattle and horses — well watered with navigated rivers full of fish — and the coast has a great number of crocodiles and tortoises. Its commodities are hides sugar rum indigo cotton cocoa coffee ginger tobacco, salt wax honey amber-grease and various kinds of drugs and dying woods. It has mines of gold silver and copper not now cultivated.[14]

o   o   o   o   o

236

In 1690 France had a fleet in the port of Brest superior to the united naval force of England and Holland —

At a certain period the French navy consisted of 115 sail of

12. *Ibid.*, I, 810–11, entry "France."
13. *Ibid.*, I, 811, entry "France." Also, in *Savary*, I, 102, entry "Rouen."
14. *Postlethwayt*, I, 826. Most of this information in *Savary*, I, 507–10, entry "Saint-Domingue, and La Tortue."

the line from 1st to fourth rates and 24 frigates etc. the whole having 7,080 pieces of cannon — 20,618 sailors and 10,904 mariners —[15]

Lewis the 14th in June 1700 established the Council of Commerce consisting of some of the principal officers of State and twelve merchants chosen and paid by the principal trading towns, to represent all things relative to trade and manufactures and propose regulations etc. — Infinite good has resulted to France from this institution. The salaries are about 400 stg per annum.[16]

o o o o o

Austria

Produces corn wine iron steel salt parts of it fruit, cattle horses — great quantity of saffron — It has a port in the Adriatic Sea called Trieste with a good harbour the chief export is iron and some salt — A good deal of wine is raised in the neighborhood — At Tirol there are mines of Iron Silver and copper which produce a good revenue to government. Schwatz is noted for mines of silver. Halle the second city of Tyrol is famous for the produce of salt 40 years before Post [lethwayt?]: According to Addison it made 3.200,00 weight and gave a revenue to the Emperor of 200,000 crowns — a great quantity of specie is coined here.

At Roveredo is a considerable manufacture of silk.[17]

o o o o o

237

The Netherlands.

Have valuable woolen manufactures but their chief manufactures are lace cambricks lawns and linnen. They have valuable manufactures of silk as well in the Austrian as in the French Netherlands.

15. *Postlethwayt*, I, 837, entry "France," where the last sentence appears: "20618 mariners, 10904 soldiers."

16. *Ibid.*, I, 832, entry "France"; also in *Savary*, II, 584–87, entry "Conseil de Commerce."

17. *Postlethwayt*, I, 157–58, entry "Austria."

Bruges (part of Aust. N.) has the most foreign trade of any town in Flanders. It is about eight miles from Ostend.[18]

The Emperor attempted here at the instance of some English Merchants to establish an East India Company which appeared to be in a thriving way — He made an alliance with Spain to support his project; but a counter alliance being formed between France England Prussian Holland and Hanover which at length obliged him to renounce it —[19]

o   o   o   o   o

The Austrian Netherlands export annually in fine thread bone lace linnen lawns and cambrick to amount of near two millions sterling besides which they export considerable quantity of tapestry woolen stuff cotton silk etc.[20] The Kingdom of Bohemia is divided into three parts — Bohemia proper Silesia and Moravia — it is bounded by Austria, Brandenburgh and Lusatia, Bavaria, Saxony and Poland — Its revenues are computed at 12 or 1400,000£ one year with another. It has the best mines in Europe both for gold and precious stones — besides its mines of silver copper tin, iron lead sulphur and nitre. The precious stones are carbuncles, emeralds, amethysts, jasper, sapphire and some others — They make salt and alum in abundance. The soil produces a great deal of saffron. They have plenty of horses and cattle, a great deal of beer but little wine. Prague is the principal city of Bohemia, the principal part of the commerce[21]

o   o   o   o   o

238

of which is carried on by the Jews — Carlsbadt another town is famous for baths and medicinal waters — it has a good many manufactures in iron —[22] Hungary in longitude 16 to 23 latitude

18. *Ibid.*, I, 158–59 entry "Austrian Netherlands." Postlethwayt's statement is as follows: "*Bruges*, a city and port-town in *Austrian Flanders*, situated 11 miles east of *Ostend*. . . ."

19. *Ibid.*, I, 159.

20. *Ibid.*, I, 160, entry "Austrian Netherlands."

21. *Ibid.*, I, 302, entry "Bohemia."

22. *Ibid.*, I, 303, entry "Bohemia."

45 to 49 North — Bounded by the Carpathian Mountains which divide it from Poland on the North by Transylvania and Wallachia on the East by the River Drave which separates it from Sclavonia on the South and by Austria and Moravia on the West. It possesses a very fruitful soil great abundance of horses and cattle — corn six times as cheap as in England — It is rich in mines of gold silver and all other metals except tin — produces a plenty of excellent wines particularly the celebrated Tockay — in some places are found even diamonds and other precious stones — it has great plenty of white red and black marble and some fine porphyry — It has a good breed of buffaloes which are made use of in husbandry — The peasants in tilling the ground find grains of gold.[23]

o o o o o

It has few other manufactures than those of copper and other hard wares — though some late attempts have been made to introduce others and with an appearance of success —

This country abounds with salutary hot baths and fountains of vitriolic petrifying and other peculiar qualities; its rivers abound with fish, a thousand carp have been sold for a crown —

Chremnitz has the finest gold mine in Europe which has been worked near a thousand years — it extends nine or ten miles in length. It has also a mine of vitriol not far from the gold mine —[24]

Shemnitz has six silver mines which also afford gold — Hewsol and Hermgrant have abundance of rich copper mines from which are also extracted silver with several sorts of vitriol. There is said to be in the last two springs of vitriolic water which have the singular faculty of turning iron[25]

o o o o o

239

into copper. There are many fine medicinal baths —[26]

23. *Ibid.*, 962, entry "Hungary." Also in *Rolt*, entry "Hungary."
24. *Rolt*, entry "Hungary."
25. *Postlethwayt*, I, 962, entry "Hungary."
26. *Ibid.*, I, 962, entry "Hungary."

35

America

Its boundaries yet unascertained — The part known little less in extent than all the other three parts together — contains the greatest part of their productions and a variety of others peculiar to itself.

After the Spaniards (says Postlethwaite) the English have the most flourishing colonies, both with regard to the multitude of the inhabitants, the number of ships they send thither every year and the rich and precious commodities they draw from them above half the trade and navigation of Great Britain being reasonably supposed to depend on her American settlement.[27]

o o o o o

240

Mesnagers in his secret memoirs says that when he returned with an account to Lewis 14th that the Spaniards would not come into his project for attacking Jamaica, the Monarch was much chagrined at their refusal and said "They were the most stupid wise people in the world."[28]

o o o o o

Asia.

Productions; all those in Europe with the addition of many either in greater abundance than there or not produced there at all —

There is a great abundance of diamons pearl coral gold silver copper, iron, sulphur red earth, salt-petre, allum quicksilver, potter's earth (of which is made the porcelain) raw silk cotton, tea, sage, coffee, nutmegs, mace cloves cinnamon pepper, indigo china-root, aquila-wood, rhubarb, musk, vermilion, sticklack borax, *lapis lazuli* Dragon's blood, cubebs frankincense, saffron myrrh, manna, ambergrease and many other of the valuable drugs and gums —

27. *Postlethwayt,* I, 55, entry "America." Also, Rolt, entry "America."
28. *Postlethwayt,* I, 377, entry "British America."

o o o o o

241

There is an immense canal in China 1000 miles long which traverses the whole Chinese empire from Canton to Pekin.[29]

There is an immense wall of 600 leagues long that is a barrier against the tartars.[30]

Asia Minor Islands.

Tenedos is famed for its excellent Muscadine wines.

Lesbos since called Mytilene besides corn wine fruit has quarries of jasper and several sorts of marble.

Chios now Scio-the rendezvous of the ships that go Constantinople or from thence to Syria Egypt etc — It has corn wine and fruit — variety of gums — some silk and other manufactures.[31]

Samos, extremely fertile, produces muscadine wine — raw silk saffron minerals drugs of different sorts — badly inhabited at present.[32]

o o o o o

Icaria, now Nicaria has no great advantages either physical or improved —

Patmos has the best port in the Archipelago nothing else remarkable.

Claros nothing worth notice.

Leria produces aloes —

Coos or Cos — one of the most flourishing of these islands produces plenty of corn wine olives and oil — has a pretty good port.

Astypata now Stampalia, not worth notice —

Carpathus, now Scarpanto — nothing remarkable here but a plenty of marble —

Rhodes, in as flourishing a state now as Turkish Government will permit besides the usual productions of corn wine oil etc.[33]

29. *Ibid.*, I, 121, entry "Asia."
30. *Ibid.*, I, 489, entry "China."
31. *Rolt*, entry "Turkish Islands, Chios."
32. *Postlethwayt*, I, 122, entry "Asia Minor Islands."
33. *Ibid.*, I, 122, entry "Asia Minor Islands."

o o o o o

242

It has iron copper and other minerals. Its manufactures are soap camblets and tapestry, damasks and other silk stuffs — it has vermilion etc.

Cyprus was formerly flourishing among other things produced sugar. This has now ceased — They have the best manufactures of cotton and wool of all the East.[34]

o o o o o

Postlethwait on funds.

"It is computed (says he) by the British Merchant that out of 49.000.000 £ expended and consumed by our people at home, not more than four millions are of foreign commodities — There remain therefore 45.000.000 £ for our annual expense and consumption in home product and manufactures. Of these the land owner can expend and consume no more than his rents, and they are computed at no more than 14.000.000 of sterling; therefore above two parts in three in home product and manufactures are expended and consumed by all other denominations of our people." He infers that the farmer and trader pay three fourths of the public taxes. . . .[35]

The circulation was about thirty millions at this time twelve in specie, eighteen in paper —

o o o o o

243

The same British Merchant in 1713 computed the imports of Great Britain at 5.000.000 £ its exports at 7000.000.[36]

Labour — "It has been judged by experience that the labour of 25 persons is nearly sufficient to provide meal drink apparel housing and generally all the necessaries of life for 100 persons." The par between land and labour is twice the quantity of land whose product will maintain the labourer. In France one acre and

34. *Ibid.*, I, 123, entry "Asia Minor Islands."
35. *Ibid.*, I, 879–80, entry "Funds."
36. *Ibid.*, I, 880, entry "Funds."

a half will maintain one in England three owing to the difference in the manner of living.[37]

o o o o o

Egypt.

Produces in abundance corn wine rice dates senna cassia baulm physical drugs plants etc.

Alexandria is now called Scanderic by the Turks — it has a considerable manufacture of striped and coarse linnen. Damietta has a very flourishing manufacture of fine linnen cloth of all colors —

Maquilla carries on several kinds of linnen and cotton manufactures — makes great quantities of sal armoniac.

Cairo is the capital of Egypt formerly a place of great trade the medium of all the commerce between Europe and the East Indies — it now carries a good many manufactures —[38]

o o o o o

244a*

particularly one of Turkey carpets. Fium a large and populous city; its principal commerce consists in linnen plain and striped, fine leather, carpets the finest mats in all Egypt, fig raisins oranges lemons and other fruits —

Upper Egypt among other things produces Rice.

Minio famous for an earthen manufacture of water potts curiously wrought and said to give a peculiar freshness to the water —

Aboutic produces vast quantities of black poppies from which the best opium is made and spread over the whole Turkish dominions.[39]

o o o o o

p. 244

Amyanthus a kind of incombustible stone said to be found in

37. *Ibid.*, II, 2, 6, entry "Labour."

38. *Ibid.*, I, 697–98, entry "Egypt."

* This page appears in the *Pay Book* before the note on Venice, and is numbered as 244a. Its natural place is here however.

39. *Postlethwayt*, I, 698, entry "Egypt."

the Isle of Cyprus and in the Pyrrhennes whose fibres resemble cotton and may be manufactured — It is pretended that the ancients made their bays in which they used to burn their dead of this stone — and that they also made paper of it which being put into the fire lost the stain of former writing — The Caravanjiers in travelling through the burning deserts of Lybia have stockings and drawers of this — some assert that it is a tric — It is also called Asbestos and is found in several other parts of the world — in India Japan China Egypt Negropont Corsica Leguria Bavaria Wales etc.

In some experiments before the Royal Society, it was found to be

o o o o o

diminished by fire; it has been vitrified by a burning glass but it cannot be consumed or calcined. It appears to be a kind of half mineral half vegetable grows in our highlands.[40]

Florence in Italy subject to the Duke of Tucany — it produces abundance of wines citrons lemons oranges olives etc. corn rice saffron honey wax wood flax hemp silk copper iron allum marble porphyry and other fine stones.

It manufactures serges and several other kinds of woolen cloths, silks linnen tapestries, gilt leather, earthen ware and perfumes.

From England it takes pepper cloves mace indico callicoes lead, tin cloths bays, perpetuanas herrings white and red, pickled salmon — Newfoundland fish pilchards calf-skins and [divers other commodities.][41]

o o o o o

Venice.

The revenues of the state of Venice were 4.000.000 ounces of silver per annum. All transactions for above a certain value were invalid if not paid in Bank.[42]

40. *Ibid.*, I, 56, entry "Amiantus," and 119–20, entry "Asbestos."

41. *Ibid.*, 799, entry "Florence." The last line of the page has been cut off, and the text within the brackets has been supplied from *Postlethwayt*.

42. *Postlethwayt*, II, 820, entry "Venice."

The Azores belong to the Portuguese 7 in number they produce corn wine fruits of every sort lie in the Atlantic Ocean between 37 + 40 N.L.[43]

The Canaries belong to Spain — Twelve in N°. of which Teneriffe one — They produce wine corn and a variety of fruits but not enough corn for their subsistence — This is the rendezvous of the galleons etc from South America.[44]

o   o   o   o   o

245

Landed Interest

Maitland in his history of London says in the year 961 land sold at 1/ per acre — in the year 1000 an ox sold for 2/6 a cow for 2/ a sheep for 1/ and a hog for 8d.

"It is agreed by the best authors of Political Arithmetic that the rents of lands houses and mines are not more than 3/8 of the annual expences of the nation."[45] Davenant calculates them at 14 millions stg.

In William Petty supposes every person in England upon an average spends 7£ a head which supposing the nation to be 7 millions makes the whole expence and consumption 49 millions."[46]

o   o   o   o   o

"Aristotles politics Chap. 6. Definition of money — As all useful things (says he) could not without great difficulty be transported from place to place, it was resolved, by common consent, that in bartering commodities they should reciprocally give and receive some substance, which being in its nature applicable to

43. *Ibid.,* I, 163, entry "Azores Islands."

44. *Ibid.,* I, 444–45, entry "Canary Islands."

45. *Ibid.,* II, 11–12, entry "Landed Interest."

46. The quoted statement is as follows: ". . . it is agreed by the best authors of political arithmetic, that the rents of lands, houses, and mines, are not more than 1/4 part, and half of the annual expences of the nation." *Ibid.,* II, 12.

the purposes of life might at the same time be easily carried about."[47]

The proportion of gold and silver as settled by Sir Isaac Newton's proposition was 1 to 14 —[48] it was generally throughout Europe 1 to 15.[49] In China I believe it is 1 to 16.[50]

o o o o o

246

It is estimated that the labour of 25 persons on an average will maintain an hundred in all the necessaries of life.[51]

Postlethwaite in his time supposes six millions of people in England —

"The ratio of increase has been found by a variety of observations to be that 100.000 people augment annually one year with another to 100.175."

"W. Kerseboom agreeing with Doctor Halley makes the number of people thirty five times the number of births in a year."[52]

o o o o o

Postlethwaite makes the Nobility Gentry Merchants Farmers Manufacturers and others which compose the increasing stock of the nation at . . . . 3.052.083.
The common soldiers seamen laboring people and   2.947.917.
out-servants cottagers paupers, vagrants, beggars ————
etc.   6.000.000 [53]

Spain produces corn wine oil all the fruits of Europe and

47. *Ibid.*, II, 282, entry "Money." Also, *Rolt,* entry "Money."

48. *Postlethwayt,* I, 528, entry "Coin." Newton's statement, as quoted by Postlethwayt, is as follows: ". . . a pound weight of fine gold will be worth 14 pounds weight, 11 ounces, 12 penny weights, 9 grains fine silver bullion." *Ibid.*

49. *Ibid.*, II, 282, entry "Money." Also, *Rolt,* entry "Money."

50. *Postlethwayt,* I, 528, entry "Coin." Here Hamilton is mistaken. Newton's statement on China reads as follows: "In China and Japan, one pound weight of fine gold is worth but 9 to 10 pounds weight of fine silver." *Ibid.*

51. *Ibid.*, II, 6, entry "Labour."

52. *Ibid.*, II, 438, entry "People."

53. *Ibid.*, II, 438, entry "People."

America the finest wool in the world and silk in abundance of which two articles there are valuable manufactures. She has mines of gold silver copper iron lead and Mercury and allum — marble in abundance."[54]

o　o　o　o　o

247

and several precious stones —[55] some provinces produce rice and sugar.[56]

The mines of South America according to the registers of the Council of Trade are said in the first hundred years to have yielded in gold silver diamonds pearls and other precious stones to the amount of 5 000.000.000 of money.[57] Arragon Valencia Estramadura and Granada are earthly paradises.[58]

Portugal is in its greatest extent from North to South 300 miles from East to West 120 — not very fertile in general — does not afford a sufficiency of corn for its own consumption produces wine and oil — the latter not good — has mines of allum white marble.[59]

o　o　o　o　o

white allum and alabaster and great quantities of salt — they have some woolen manufactures but of no value. Some silk but of inferior quality.[60]

Russia commodities for exportation are Pitch Tar, in great quantity

Honey and bees wax

Russia leather deer bear and elkskins

Pot-ash timber and plank iron and some copper.

Hemp and flax, linseed the best in Europe

Linnen and linnen yarn, Russia linnen

54. *Ibid.,* II, 750, entry "Spain."
55. *Ibid.,* II, 750, entry "Spain."
56. *Ibid.,* II, 752, entry "Spain."
57. *Ibid.,* II, 761, entry "Spanish America."
58. *Ibid.,* II, 751–53, entry "Spain."
59. *Ibid.,* II, 507, entry "Portugal."
60. *Ibid.,* II, 507, entry "Portugal."

Furrs such as sable black fox ermine raindeer martins beaver
Raw silk by the Wolga
Persian Indian and Chinese goods
Deals firr timber masts
corn sturgeon and cavear
Diaper[61]

o o o o o

248

Sail cloth canvas and duck
Pot-ash.
Tobacco in plenty from Circassia,
Salt — very rich mines —
The Russian general export from Petersburgh estimated at three millions of which two by British subjects — The English had a million ballance against them.[62]

The native exports of Portugal are wine lemons oranges figs raisins almonds salt oil cork shumac tunny fish and other small articles — some wool is also exported though prohibited.

The commodities they bring from their foreign dominions are diamonds of Brazil and India, sugar tobacco Brazil wood cocoanuts coffee cotton pepper drugs.[63]

o o o o o

Some inferior spices, whalebone raw and tanned hides, elephants teeth arrac orchella citrons and occasionally china ware. India silks and cotton piece goods — Silver and gold the former by surmission obtaining license the latter candestenely.[64]

Venice has the largest state of any in the Mediterranean —

61. *Ibid.*, II, 642, entry "Russia." Also, Rolt, entry "Russia."

62. *Postlethwayt*, II, 642–49, entry "Russia." In *Rolt*, entry "Russia," there is the following statement: "According to Mr. Hamway, the ordinary annual computation of the Russian general export from St. Petersburg is three millions of rubles, or 675,000 l. Sterling, of which the British subjects in Russia take off 2 millions, or 450,000 l. Sterling."

63. *Postlethwayt*, II, 512, entry "Portugal." Also, Rolt, entry "Portugal."

64. *Postlethwayt*, II, 513, entry "Portugal." Also, Rolt, entry "Portugal."

she possesses Dalmatia and several islands in the neighborhood
of the Morea. Her land is not very abundant in its productions
nor has she many manufactures but she is the mart of that part of
the world — she has a large inland commerce by the River Po the
Addige Adda etc —[65]

o   o   o   o   o

249

She has some silk manufactures. She has some mines of iron and
lead all sorts of naval stores. She imports great quantities of
drugs from her neighbours, which she sells again to the rest of
the world — she had the finest glass manufactories in the world
but was rivalled by France who has been since rivalled by England. There is a good deal of luxury at Venice — which is of service to her by an influx of strangers.[66]

o   o   o   o   o

Extracts from Demosthenes Orations

Philippic 1 — "As a general marches at the head of his troops,
so ought wise politicians, if I dare use the expression, to march
at the head of affairs; insomuch that they ought not to wait the
event, to know what measures to take; but the measures which
they have taken, ought to produce the *event*"[67]

"Where attack him it will be said? Ah Athenians war, war itself will discover to you his weak sides, if you seek them."
Sublimely Simple. Vide Long: C[hapter] 16.[68]

o   o   o   o   o

65. *Postlethwayt,* II, p. 819, entry: "Venice."

66. *Ibid.,* II, 819–20, entry "Venice."

67. This frequently mentioned statement, as expressing a Hamiltonian
concept of leadership, constitutes a liberal translation of Demosthenes' *First
Philippic,* 39–40.

68. The reference given by Hamilton is not correct. The quotation is not
from Longinus, but from Demosthenes' *First Philippic,* 44, 16–19. Longinus,
quoting the same paragraph for an aesthetic analysis in his *On the Sublime,*
XVIII, I, 10–12, omitted several words of the original; thus, he omitted the
"Ah Athenians" of Hamilton's translation; instead of "his weak sides," Longinus has "the weak sides of Phillip," and he also omitted the last four
words, "if you seek them."

[250A]

Are the limits of the several states and the arts on which they are founded ascertained and are our ministers provided with them?

What intelligence has been given to Congress by our ministers of the designs strength by sea and land, actual interests and views of the different powers in Europe?

o   o   o   o   o

[251A]

These notes are selected more for their singularity than use — though some important facts are comprehended —[69]

o   o   o   o   o

252

Plutarch's Lives

Vol. 1

Theseus — Aegeus (his father) "being desirous of children consulted the oracle at Delphi and received that celebrated answer which forbad him the use of any woman before his return to Athens" — It was in these words

> "The mystic vessel must untouched remain
> 'Till thou to Athens shalt return again"

Page II. "Procrustes a robber of Attica slain by Theseus in the same manner he used to put to death those who fell into his hands —

He had beds of several sizes and when he lit upon a traveller

69. The following notes of Hamilton through manuscript page 276 constitute a liberal translation and frequently an outlined version of parts from four of Plutarch's Lives: Theseus, Romulus, Lycurgus, and Numa Pompilius. It is not clear what text Hamilton did use. There are several similarities between his notes and those of a Dryden translation of the Lives printed in six volumes by Alexander Donaldson of Edinburgh, in 1774. However, alterations in spelling, a few different words, and the numbering of paragraphs exclude this edition as well as other editions frequently used in Hamilton's time, such as North's translation from the French of Amyott, Dyer's, Langhorne's and others.

The number at the beginning of paragraphs probably corresponds to the pagination of the original text as shown by the note on manuscript page 272.

if he was too tall he would cut off a part of his legs, if too short he would extend him by machines to fit his beds.[70]

Minos the king of the Cretans reduced the Athenians so low that by advice of the oracle they bound them-

o   o   o   o   o

Theseus

selves every ninth year to pay a tribute of seven young men and seven virgins, who the fable says were put into a subterraneous place and there devoured by an animal called the Minotaur. Soon after Theseus arrived at Athens, the time of the tribute came about. He went a volunteer contrary to the persuasions of his father Aegeus; and by the assistance of Ariadne the daughter of Minos who fell in love with him, he slew the Minotaur and returned with the young men and virgins triumphant to Athens, bringing off Ariadne with him. It is added that if he returned safe there was a convential signal to be hoisted on the vessel, which in the hurry of his joy was omitted — Aegeus in sorrow for he imagined loss of

o   o   o   o   o

253

his son precipitated himself from a rock into the sea.

26. Theseus is said to have instituted games at Delos and to have been the introducer of the custom of giving palms to victors.

70. The legend of Procrustes must have impressed Hamilton greatly. Years later, he referred to this legend on several occasions. For instance, in an article in the *American Daily Advertiser*, February 1, 1794, in which he attacked the attitude of Jefferson and Madison toward the French Revolution, Hamilton wrote: "They observe that among these a Marat and a Robespierre, assassins still reeking with the blood of their fellow-citizens, monsters who outdo the fabled enormities of a *Busiris* and a *Procrustes,* are predominant in influence as well as iniquity." *Lodge,* V, 76–77. In a Cabinet Paper written from Philadelphia on August 18, 1792, answering the objections against the new government made by Colonel George Mason, at the instigation, probably, of Thomas Jefferson, Hamilton again implied the Procrustes myth when he said: "Every man who is either too short or too long for your political couch must be stretched or lopped to suit it."—*Ibid.,* II, 455.

33. Hercules in honor of Jupiter instituted the Olympian games; in imitation of him Theseus instituted the Isthmian games in honor of Neptune —

He was the first that divided the commonwealth into three ranks, the nobles, the husbandmen and Artificers; to the first he committed the care of religion the choice of Magistrates the interpreting and dispencing the laws —

"Theseus was the first as Aristotle says who out of inclination to popular government parted with the regal power."

Castor and Pollux were two brothers whose sister having been ravished by Theseus took Athens in his absence.

o   o   o   o   o

They were worshipped afterwards as gods for the care they took of the city. "His tomb was placed near the gymnasium and is a sanctuary for servants and others in distress, thereby signifying that while living he was the patron of the poor and afflicted.

In his absence from Athens his wife Phædra fell violently in love with his son Hyppolitus who was banished by his father in consequence of the resentment of Phædra and was devoured by a sea Monster — This fable has given rise to the Tragedy of Phædra by Euripides imitated by Racine — the conduct and execution of which piece are as admirable as the subject is monstrous disgusting and absurd.

o   o   o   o   o

254

The Athenians sacrifice to Theseus the eighth day of every month, in the same manner as they do to Neptune whose reputed son he was — The mythical meaning of this sacrifice is "because the number 8 being the first cube of an even number and the double of the first square, seemed to be an emblem of the immovable power of this god, who has the names of *Asphalius* and Gaieochus the establisher and supporter of the earth."

o   o   o   o   o

Romulus[71]

52: One of the accounts of his origin is that Tarchetius King of Alba saw in his own house the apparition of the God Priapus issuing out of the chimney hearth — and having consulted the oracle was told, that some young virgin should accept the embraces of the God and that she should have a son eminent for strength valour and good fortune. He commanded one of his own daughters to entertain the lover but she thinking it an indignity sent her servant maid in her place who some time after brought two sons Romulus and Remus etc etc. The most received is the story of the vestal virgin well known etc.

54: The Romans call the tutela goddess of young children Rumilia and in sacrificing to her use milk instead of wine in their libation.

o o o o o

255

54. The keeper of Hercules's temple having it seems little else to do proposed to his deity a game at dice on condition that if he won he should have something valuable of the god, and if he lost he would provide him with a good supper and a pretty girl. Having lost he kept his word and Larentia was the woman — to whom as the mistress of a god sacred honors were afterwards paid.

The vulture was a favourite omen with the ancients because says Plutarch "it is the least hurtful of any animal; it preys only upon carrion and never kills or molests any living animal; and as for birds it touches not them, though dead, as being of its own species."

o o o o o

64. The city being built, Romulus inlisted all that were able to bear arms into military companies of 3000 footmen and 300 horse; which were called legions because they were the choicest and most select of the people. An hundred of the most eminent men

71. The next nine pages constitute outlined notes of Plutarch's Life of Romulus. It seems that Hamilton here has kept in an outline form comments on Plutarch's text made by an unknown annotator.

49

he chose for his counsellors who were styled patricians and the whole body of them the senate which signifies a consistory of old men.

The senate were afterwards called *patres* and then *patres conscripti* to distinguish them from the populace. A relation was established between the nobles and the common people in this manner the former were styled patrons and the latter clients. Every common man chose some nobleman for his client and a

o   o   o   o   o

256

reciprocity of good offices was established.

The patrons were the counsellors and pleaders for their clients in law suits, their advocates when under prosecution their advisers and directors in all affairs — These in return were warmly attached to their patrons, not only showed them great respect and deference but supported their interests and in case of poverty helped them to portion their daughters and pay their debts. No law could oblige a patron to be witness against his client or the client against his patron.

78. When the accommodation took place between Romulus and Tatius uniting the Romans and Sabins an hundred Sabin Senators were elected and the legions were increased to 6000 foot and 600 horse; the

o   o   o   o   o

whole people were divided into three tribes, each tribe containing ten curiæ or wards —

The commentator says Plutarch was mistaken in the number of the Legion, and asserts from Livy's authority that during the reign of Romulus it never consisted of more than three thousand foot and 300 horse — that after the kings they were augmented to 4000 foot again to 5000 and lastly by Scipio Africanus to 6000 — and the horse to 600 —

Romulus adopted the use of the Sabin shields instead of the small Roman targets — The feasts and sacrifices of both nations were united and new ones introduced the Matronalia and Carmentalia; the former in honor of the women for having put an end to the war. Carmenta is thought by

o o o o o

257

some to be the destiny who presides over child-birth — By others she is said to have been a priestess who delivered her oracles in verse —

In the feasts of the Lupercalia two young noblemen were produced — a bloody knife was applied to their forheads and the blood was afterwards wiped off by wool dipped in milk — Then the two young men run about naked and with thongs of goat skin whipped all they met. The young married women were glad of this kind of whipping as they imagined it helped conception —

Some say that Romulus instituted the order of vestals though the most received account of his birth makes his mother a vestal — others ascribe the institution to Numa. Romulus as Pontifex maximus had a lituus[72]

o o o o o

rod used in describing the four quarters of the heavens in auguries from the flight of birds — This lituus after Rome was sacked and burnt by the Gauls is pretended to have been found unhurt amongst the ruins. A trick of Camillus's to encourage the citizens to rebuild the city instead of going to Veic as they wanted —

A husband might put away his wife for three causes adultery poisoning her children and counterfeiting his keys —

It is said that Romulus having taken the city of Fidenæ made it a Roman colony and sent there 2500 inhabitants.

Having soon after overcome the Camerians he removed those

o o o o o

258

who survived to Rome and soon after sent back double the number — This was 16 years after the foundation —

Romulus after having subdued all his enemies abroad grew haughty and affected absolute government. He established the

72. An augur's crook.

lectors who preceded him with rods and leather thongs to bing [bind?] whom he should direct.

92. Plutarch speaking against the translation of human bodies to heaven adopts the sentiment of Pindar in these lines

"Our bodies shrink to dust by deaths decree
the soul survives and feels eternity"—

He says, "We must not contrary to nature send the bodies with the souls of good men to heaven; but then we must readily believe, that both from

o o o o o

their nature and the divine constitution virtuous souls are exalted from men into heroes, from heroes into demigods, and after that, if they are perfectly purified as in the sacred initiation and refined from all the passions which attend mortality, they are raised to consummate felicity and enrolled amongst the gods, not by the vote of a people, but by the just and established order of nature."

Hesiod is said to have originated these four distinctions — Plato has similar ideas in that philosophic fiction of a regular gradation of beings from nothing to infinite; a scheme as inconsistent with fact as sublime in theory — Shaftesbury among the moderns revived it and Pope has erected a delightful poem upon this foundation.[73]

o o o o o

259

give up any part of his prerogative. Whoever gives up his right, or extends his claim too far, is no more a king but either a slave to the people or a tyrant and so becomes odious or contemptible to his subjects. The one seems to be the fault of easiness and good nature, the other of pride and severity" A false sentiment; it would often be praise worthy in a prince to relinquish a part of an excessive prerogative to establish a more moderate government, better adapted to the happiness or temper of his people.

73. It seems that between this and page numbered 259 were one or more pages, now lost.

Plutarch pronounces a very harsh sentence upon Theseus on the occasion of his having omitted to hoist the signal agreed upon by his father though the omission was only an inadvertiness —[74]

o   o   o   o   o

98. He says "But Theseus in his forgetfulness of the command concerning the flag can scarcely in my opinion by any excuses, or before the mildest judges avoid the imputation of Paricide"— This shows in how high veneration the commands of a father were held.

Lycurgus.[75]

107. He met with the works of Homer in Ionia and transcribed and collected them. He is said to have been the first that brought them into general reputation.

In his travels to see the government and manners of different countries — he passed into Egypt and "being much pleased with their

o   o   o   o   o

260

way of separating their soldiery from the rest of the people he resolved to imitate them at Lacedæmon; and this distinction of the military men from those of low and mechanical employments rendered the constitution much more regular and beautiful."

Lycurgus being returned to Sparta resolved to new model the commonwealth and having consulted the oracle concerning it — the propetess called him "beloved of the gods and rather a god than a man" assuring him that the laws he should establish would make the commonwealth which observed them the most famous in the world.

Sparta had originally two kings — Archelaus one of them said of his partner when he heard him

o   o   o   o   o

74. On the next two pages Hamilton returned to the Life of Theseus in order to note Plutarch's harsh opinion on Theseus' forgetfulness.

75. The pages to 272 include outlined parts of Plutarch's Life of Lycurgus as well as remarks made probably by another commentator.

highly extolled for his goodness "How can Charilaus be a good man who cannot be severe even to the worst of men."

109 "Amongst the many Alterations which Lycurgus made, the first and most important was the establishment of the Senate which having a power equal to the Kings in matters of consequence did (as Plato expresses it) soften and qualify the imperious and fiery genius of Monarchy, by constantly restraining it within the bounds of equity and moderation. For the state before had no firm basis to stand upon, leaning sometimes towards an absolute monarchy and sometimes towards a pure democracy; but this establishment of the senate was to the commonwealth what the ballast is

o   o   o   o   o

261

to a ship and preserved the whole in a just equilibrium. For they always adhered to the kings so far as to oppose a democracy and on the other side attested the people to prevent tyranny."

The having two kings, the senate and the Ephore are considered by Aristotle, as the causes of the duration of the Spartan government. The first circumstance would be in modern times a source of endless confusion and distraction.

The principal regulations of the Spartan government were the ordinances of the oracles called Rhetræ — one of them is in the following terms "After you have built a temple to Jupiter the Syllanian and to Minerva the Syllanian and after you have divided the people

o   o   o   o   o

into tribes and classes, you shall establish a council of thirty senators in the number of which the two kings shall be comprised and you shall from time to time call the people to an assembly betwixt Babyca and Cnacion and they shall have the supreme power of determination.

The Senate proposed and the people adopted or rejected; they could not alter or add. Finding they departed from this rule, a Rhetra was procured decreeing "that if the people should alter or pervert any law, then the senate and kings should reject it"—

However careful Lycurgus was to temper the constitution, it is said the power of the kings and senate was found to be too great and sometimes oppressive, which induced Theopompus one of their kings

o   o   o   o   o

262

to establish the Ephori. These were five in number chosen among the people for a year. Their authority was very extensive.

Theopompus when his queen upbraided him one way that he would leave the regal power to his children less than he had received it from his ancestors replied that he would leave it greater because more durable.[76]

o   o   o   o   o

For the prerogative being thus kept within reasonable bounds were secured both from envy and dangers.

The most arduous and dangerous thing attempted by Lycurgus was the division of property which when he began was very unequal. The lands and money were in the hands of a few and there were a great number of necessitous people. "Therefore that he might banish out of the commonwealth luxury and arrogance and erring and fraud, together with those more fatal and inveterate distempers of a state, wealth and poverty, he persuaded the people to reduce the whole country to a common stock to consent to a new division of the land, and live all in perfect equality allowing the pre-eminence to virtue only and considering

o   o   o   o   o

263

no other difference or inequality between one man and another,

76. On June 21, 1788, Hamilton in his speech at the New York Convention for the ratification of the United States Constitution, remarked: "I could illustrate the position by a variety of historical examples both ancient and modern. In Sparta, the Ephori were a body of magistrates, instituted as a check upon the Senate and representing the people. They consisted of only five men; but they were able to protect their rights and therefore enjoyed their confidence and attachment."—*Lodge*, II, 22–23.

but what the disgrace of doing base actions or credit of doing worthily created" — He divided the whole country of Laconia into thirty thousand shares and the territory of the city of Sparta into 9 thousand and made the distribution. A lot was so much as to yield one year with another seventy bushels of grain for the master of the family and twelve for his wife with a proportion of wine and fruits. The whole population this ground could support could not much exceed 600,000.

To destroy avarice he cried down all the gold and silver and made only iron currents.

"He instituted public tables at which every citizen was obliged to eat — there were different

o   o   o   o   o

messes. No man could be admitted into any mess but by unanimous consent.

The Rich were so enraged at Lycurgus that a tumult arose one day and a young man run after him and knocked out one of his eyes. He carried the young man home with him and instead of punishing him as he was authorised to do made him one of his most zealous partisans by kindness —

The principal dish of the Lacedemonians was a kind of blackbroth which the old men fed solely upon by preference. A king of Pontus sent for a Lacedemonian cook, to make him some black broth.

o   o   o   o   o

264

Finding it very disagreeable on tasting it — The cook observed to him "In [order] to make this broth relish you must first bath yourself in the Eurotas —"

By one of his Rhetræ Lycurgus forbid his laws being written imagining that the impressing would be more lasting and efficacious by obliging the citizens to depend on their memory, than by referring them to a written code.

Another of the Rhetræ ordained that only the saw and the ax should be used in their buildings — This was to prevent luxury in building furniture etc. — For as Epaminondas afterwards said of his table "Treason will never come to such a dinner as this;" So Lycurgus thought

O O O O O

that such houses would never be the receptacles of luxury and superfluity.

Another Rhetra ordained that they should not make war often along with the same enemy, for fear of instructing them in the art of war.

To make the women more robust and more capable of a rigorous offspring, he ordered them to practice several of the athletic exercises — and to destroy an excessive delicacy he ordained that at certain solemn feasts and sacrifices the virgins should go naked as well as the young men and in this manner dance in their presence.

The women of these occasions used to praise or rally the young

O O O O O

265

men who had done any honorable or dishonorable action, which was a great incitement to emulation.

To promote marriage those who continued batchelors beyond a certain age were made infamous by law — they were excluded from the public spectacles and the magistrates sometimes made them dance naked through the market place singing a song to their own disgrace.

124 When a couple were to be married the husband carried off the bride by force. She who was charged with the management of the wedding shaved the head of the bride dressed her in men's cloaths and left her at the place of rendezvous

O O O O O

where after the usual supper the Bridegroom came secretly in quest of her, untied her girdle and carried her to another bed. The intercourse between them continued some time privately —
125. To prevent jealousy a man might lend his wife "Lycurgus al-

lowed a man who was in years and had a young wife to recommend some virtuous handsome young man that she might have a child by him who might inherit the good qualities of such a father. On the other side a worthy man, who was in love with a married woman, *on account of her modesty*[77] and the beauty of her children was at liberty to beg of her husband's admission to her that thus by

o o o o o

266

planting in a good soil he might raise a generous progeny to possess all the valuable qualifications of their parents."

127 It was ordained that deformed and sulky children should be
128 cast into the place called Apotheta a deep cavern near the mountain Taygetus, to prove the strength of their constitutions the women used to bath the new born children in wine instead of water; imagining that epyleptic and weakly children would die in the operation and only the vigorous and healthy survive. The principle was that it was neither for the good of the public nor of the child itself that it should be preserved when nature had denied it the means of happiness health and strength. A horrid practice mentioned with no mark of disapprobation.

o o o o o

Every lad had a lover or friend who took care of his education and shared in the praise or blame of his virtues or vices. It was the same with the women.

129 The youth were educated to theft, to give them habits of courage and address. If taken in the fact the person was severely whipped for his negligence and want of dexterity. The youth were accustomed to spare diet to stimulate their enterprise in this way and promote their health. Plutarch has this remark "But there was another subordinate intention which was to make them grow tall; for the vital spirits not being overburthened and oppressed by too great a quantity of nourishment (which necessarily extends itself into thickness

77. Hamilton's emphasis.

O   O   O   O   O

267

and breadth) do by their natural lightness and activity mount upwards so that the body while it is pliable and yielding must necessarily increase in length" — a kind of jargon which only shoes [shows] the ignorance of the times in the science of the human frame.

130. Tis said that a young Lacedæmonian having stolen a fox, and put it under his cloak suffered it to tear out his bowels rather than be detected in the fact.

It was primitively a custom to sacrifice a man to Diana Taurian every year which sacrifice was abolished by Lycurgus and her Goddessship was obliged to content herself with the blood of the boys who had been whipped round her altar.

O   O   O   O   O

The Lacedæmonians were remarkable for a laconic sententious way of speaking — Among other sayings recorded of Lycurgus are these — being consulted how best to oppose an invasion of their enemies he replied "by continuing poor and one not coveting to have more than another" — Being again consulted whether it were requisite to inclose the city with a wall he sent back word "That city is best fortified which has a wall of men instead of brick."

A stranger once said to Theopompus that he was so remarkable for his love to the Lacedæmonians as to be called from thence Philolacon (a lover of the La-d-s [Lacedæmonians]. Theopompus replied that it had been more for his honor to have been called Philopolites (a lover of his own countrymen) —

O   O   O   O   O

268

An Orator at Athens asserting that the Lacedæmonians were an illiterate and ignorant people, Plistoanax the son of Pausanias told him "You say true for we only of all the Grecians have learned none of your ill qualities."

A Spartan being asked to go to hear a man who exactly counterfeited the voice of the nightingale replied "I have heard the nightingale itself."

The Lacedæmonians erected a temple to the Muses and cultivated poetry and music with success making them subservient to moral and political purposes.

When the Spartans were at war their exercises were more moderate and their fare better; so that war to them was the season of repose and enjoyment. They always advanced to

o o o o o

battle with a hymn to Castor — when they routed the enemy they persued them no further than till they were assured of the victory, then they sounded a retreat, thinking it base to destroy those who made no resistance. This was not the practice in remote antiquity. "This conduct did not only show their magnanimity, but had an advantage in it too; for the enemy knowing that they killed only those who resisted and gave quarter to the rest generally thought it their best way to consult their safety by flight."

138. The Spartans despised all labour and mechanic arts; arms were the only honorable profession. The helotes tilled the ground and paid their masters the revenues already mentioned. "A certain Lacedæmonian

o o o o o

269

happened to be at Athens when the courts of justice were sitting, and hearing that a citizen who had been fined for idleness came home much discontented, and attended by his friends who were greatly concerned for his disgrace, the Lacedæmonian desired the company to show him the man who was condemned for living like a Gentleman."

The Spartans were so far from being morose, that Lycurgus dedicated a little statue to the god of laughter and great pleasantry prevailed in conversation —

Xenophon says it was the custom for the Ephori to appoint three officers and each of these were to pick out an hundred of the best men in the city and it was a point of great emulation to be one of these

o o o o o

140. three hundred — Pædaretus having been refused admittance into this list returned home well pleased saying "He rejoiced to find that there were in Sparta three hundred men better than himself."

The Senate were chosen for life out of men not under sixty; a wise institution. The elections were made by shoutings and persons were placed apart to number the frequency and loudness of those for each candidate.

The person chosen had two portions of food allowed him at the public tables one of which he gave to the woman he esteemed most; a great mark of distinction.

Lycurgus banished all strangers who could not give a very good account of themselves to prevent a corruption of morals and the introduction of customs

o o o o o

270

repugnant to the constitution.

143. "Hitherto (says Plutarch) I for my part can see no sign of injustice in the laws of Lycurgus though some who allow that they are well contrived for making men good soldiers, yet censure them as defective in civil justice and honesty. Perhaps it was the Cryptia or Ambuscade, if this were one of Lycurgus's institutions, as Aristotle says it was, that gave Plato likewise the same opinion both of the lawgiver and his government. The thing was this: The Magistrates dispatched from time to time some of the ablest of the young men into the Country where they dispersed themselves, being armed only with their daggers and taking a little necessary provision with them. In the daytime they hid themselves in the

o o o o o

thickets and clefts, but in the night they issued out into the highways and killed all the helots they could light upon; sometimes they set upon them by day, as they were at work in the fields and murdered the ablest and stoutest of them. And Thucidydes in his history of the Peloponnesian War tells us that such of them as the Lacedæmonians had singled out for their valour were crowned as persons infranchised and went about to all the temples in token of freedom; but that soon after they all disappeared of a sudden, being about the number of 2000 and no man either then or since could give any account how they were destroyed. Aristotle particularly says, that the Ephori as soon as they entered into their office

o   o   o   o   o

271

used to declare war against them that they might be massachred under pretence of law. In other respects too, the Spartans dealt very hardly with them; for they often forced them to drink to excess and led them in that condition into their public halls that their children might see what a contemptible vice drunkenness was. They made them sing such songs and dance such dances as were vulgar and ridiculous forbidding them to meddle with any that were liberal and graceful. Upon this account when the Thebans invaded Laconia and took a great number of the Helots prisoners, they could by no means persuade them to sing the odes of Terpander, Alcman, or Spendon the Lacedæmonian, because they said that they were forbidden by their masters."

o   o   o   o   o

After Lycurgus thought his institutions had acquired stability, he took an oath of the whole Nation to observe them till his return and set out to consult the oracle of Delphi. "Whether the laws he had established were sufficient to make a city virtuous and happy" The oracle replied "That his laws were excellent and that the city should continue in the highest renown while it observed the polity of Lycurgus." He wrote down the answer and sent it to Sparta and then that his countrymen might never be released from their oath it is said he put an end to his own life by a total abstinence from food.

The Government established by him remained in vigor about five

o o o o o

272

hundred years 'till a thirst of empire tempted the Spartans to entertain foreign troops and introduce Persian gold to maintain them; then the institutions of Lycurgus fell at once and avarice and luxury were introduced succeeded.*

o o o o o

Numa Pompilius[78]

Every generation consists of thirty years, an olympiad of forty†
155 After the death of Romulus, the Romans and Sabins not be-
156 ing able to agree on the choice of another King, came to this determination that each senator should exercise the regal power by turns six hours by day and six hours by night to prevent all jealousy and this kind of Government was called an interregnum. But the people clamouring through envy and jealousy, the Senate were obliged to come to the determination of choosing a King and they adopted the wise experience of one party choosing out of the body of the other. The choice was left to the Romans who pitched upon Numa and sent an embassy to him in his retirement to persuade him to accept the royalty. He was prevailed up with great difficulty. His answer to the ambassadors page 160 is full of

o o o o o

273

very sensible reflections. He was a wise Prince and went a great way in civilizing the romans. The chief engine he employed for this purpose was religion, which could alone have sufficient empire over the minds of a barbarous and war-like people to engage them to cultivate the arts of peace. "Numa (says Plutarch[)]

---

* The last two words have been crossed out in the Ms.

78. The pages to 276 include a liberal translation of parts from Plutarch's Life of Numa, as well as comments made probably by an editor of Plutarch's *Lives* whose edition Hamilton used.

† This note appears in the margin of the Ms.

judging that it was no slight undertaking to civilize the furious and unruly spirit of this people called in the assistance of religion and chiefly by the sacrifices processions and religious dances which he appointed, at which he officiated in person and in which an agreeable amusement was mixed with their solemn devotion he soothed the minds of the people and rendered their fiery martial temper more cool and sedate. Sometimes he filled their imaginations with religious terrors pretending that [strange apparitions had been seen, and dreadful voices heard; Thus][79] subdued their minds and rendered them submissive by superstition.["] ["]It is not improbable["] says Plutarch ["]that God who places not his affections on horses or birds but on mankind, should be pleased to dwell with such as are eminently virtuous and not disdain to converse with the wise and good, though it be altogether irrational to believe that any god or Damon is capable of a sensual love for a human bodily form or beauty; and yet the Egyptians make a distinction which seems not very absurd; they suppose that a divine spirit may possibly approach

o   o   o   o   o

a woman and produce in her the principles of generation; but on the other side that it is impossible for a man to have any such intercourse with a goddess; but at the same time they do not consider that there can be no mixture without a mutual communication."

Speaking of Zaleucus Minos Zoroaster Lycurgus Numa and others, He says "What if we should suppose that the gods make it a serious business to inspire such men with great and noble designs, and that if they ever converse with poets and musicians they do it merely to divert themselves?"

165 It is said that Pythagoras had tamed an eagle which in pronouncing certain words would come down to him sometimes

79. The sentence within the brackets, as well as the nine words that follow it, have been written in the margin of the preceding page. The text within the brackets, however, has been destroyed evidently during an amateurish attempt at binding the Pay Book.

when the people were assembled at the Olympic games he would show them a golden thigh — upon which Timon the Phileasian wrote this distich

o o o o o

274

"The Samian juggler of applause so proud —
who tries with solemn words to cheat the crowd —

In like manner, Numa feigned that a certain Goddess or Mountain nymph was in love with him and frequently met him in private —

165 "Pythagoras supposed that the supreme being was not an object of sense or capable of any suffering or infirmity, but was incorruptible invisible and to be comprehended only by the mind. And Numa forbad the romans to represent God in the form of man or beast; nor was there any picture or statue of a deity admitted among them formerly; for during the space of the first hundred and seventy years, they built temples and erected chapels but made no images, thinking that it was a great impiety to represent the most excellent beings by things so base and unworthy,

o o o o o

and that it was by the understanding only that man could form any conception of the deity.

167 The first institution of Chief Priests called Pontifices is ascribed to Numa.

The [To?] Numa is ascribed the institution of the sacred fire and the Vestal Virgins — If by any accident the fire became extinct it was relighted by burning glasses — The number of vestal virgins were six who were obliged to preserve their chastity thirty years; a violation of which subjected them to being burned alive.

"It is said also that Numa built the temple of Vesta intended for a repository of the holy fire, in an orbicular form, not with a design to represent the figure of the earth, but the frame of the Universe, in the center of which the Pythagorians place the ele-

65

ment of fire, giving it the name of Vesta or Unity; but they do not hold that the earth is immoveable or that it is situated in

o   o   o   o   o

275

the middle of the world, but that it has a circular motion about the central fire. Nor do they count the Earth among the chief or primary elements. And this they say was the opinion of Plato, who in his old age, held that the earth was placed at a distance from the center, for that being the principal place was reserved for some more noble and refined body."

172 Numa instituted the Priests called Fecialos whose office it was to judge of the merits of a war before it was entered upon and to accommodate differences. When the Romans received any injuries from their neighbours, they dispatched these priests to represent their grievances and obtain amicable redress, which being refused they denounced war. It is remarkable that the decrees of these priests upon different occasions

o   o   o   o   o

were very consistent with unbiased justice and that when their advice was not followed, the Romans generally had cause to repent it.

Numa pretended that a certain Target fell from heaven which until it was preserved would render the romans invincible. He had eleven others made exactly like it and the whole deposited in different temples, the true one in that of Minerva near her statue. These Targets were called *Ancylia.*

It is said that Numa having invited a number of citizens to an entertainment told them that the Goddess with whom he conversed was coming in and all of a sudden the whole room was changed into a more splendid and better furnished apartment.

Numa built a temple to Faith and Terminus the god of bounds

o   o   o   o   o

276

and taught the Romans that to swear by faith was the most solemn of all oaths — This was to teach them to respect their engagements and the boundaries of their neighbours —

Doctor Halley's Table of Observations exhibiting the probabilities of life – containing an account of the whole number of people at Breslau capital of Silesia, and the number of those of every age from one to an hundred –

Ages	Persons	Ages	Persons	Ages	Persons	Ages	Persons	Ages	Persons	Ages	Persons	Ages	Persons
1	1000	8	680	15	628	22	586	29	539	36	481	7	5547
2	855	9	670	16	622	23	579	30	531	37	472	14	4584
3	798	10	661	17	616	24	573	31	523	38	463	21	4270
4	760	11	653	18	610	25	567	32	515	39	454	28	3964
5	732	12	646	19	604	26	560	33	507	40	445	35	3604
6	710	13	640	20	598	27	553	34	499	41	436	42	3178
7	692	14	634	21	592	28	546	35	490	42	427	49	2709
	5547		4584		4270		3964		3604		3178	56	2194
												63	1694
												70	1204
												77	692
												84	253
												100	107
													34000
													33893

Ages	Persons	Ages	Persons	Ages	Persons	Ages	Persons	Ages	Persons	Ages	Persons
43	417	50	346	57	272	64	202	71	131	78	58
44	407	51	335	58	262	65	192	72	120	79	49
45	397	52	324	59	252	66	182	73	109	80	41
46	387	53	313	60	242	67	172	74	98	81	34
47	377	54	302	61	232	68	162	75	88	82	28
48	367	55	292	62	222	69	152	76	78	83	23
49	357	56	282	63	212	70	142	77	68	84	20
	2709		2194		1694		1204		692		253

From 84 to 100 are 107.

From this table it will appear there are 18053 persons between 18 and 56 half of whom are fencible arm bearing men more than ¼ of the whole.[80]

o o o o o

80. Postlethwayt, I, 69, entry "Annuities." Edmond Halley (1650–1742), the famous astronomer, published his first two studies on the mortality of mankind, drawn from the Breslau tables of births and deaths, in the Philosophical Transactions of the Royal Society of London, XVII, No. 196, 596–610, and No. 198, 654–656 (London, 1693).

Numa encouraged the citizens much to Agriculture and for this purpose distributed the lands into Pagi or boroughs appointing overseers to them. He would himself survey the lands reward the industrious and reprove the indolent. The people were then divided into two classes Romans and Sabins — productive of great inconveniences. He thru them into companies

o   o   o   o   o

[The next two pages (which are not printed here) contain various mathematical calculations which were possibly connected with problems placed by Postlethwayt in vol. I, pp. 69–73, entry: "Annuities."]

o   o   o   o   o

278

According to the tables of deaths and births in the same city drawn up monthly by Doctor Newman for the course of five years it appears that upon an average there were born annually 1238

buried   1174

difference   64

By the same tables it appears that 348 of the births die in the first year and that in five years afterwards 193 more die so that only 692 children survive six years.[81]

Table of deaths of different ages the first column representing the ages the second the number of person who die:[82]

Ages	7 . 8 . 9 ... 14 .... 18 ... 21 ... 27 . 28 ... 35
Persons	11 . 11 . 6 . 5½ 2 . 3½ . 5 . 6 . 4½6½ . 9 . 8 . 7 . 7

Ages	36 ... 42 ... 45 .... 49 . 54 . 55 . 56 .... 63 ....
Persons	8 . 9½ . 8.9 .. 7.7 ... 10 . 11 .. 9 .. 9 . 10 . 12 . 9½

Ages	70 . 71 . 72 ... 77 ... 81 ... 84 .... 90 : 91 . 98 . 99
Persons	14 . 9 . 11 . 9 . 6 . 7 . 3 . 4 . 2 . 1 . 1 : 1 . 0 . 1/5

Ages	100
Persons	2/5

81. There is an error in calculation copied by Hamilton from *Postlethwayt*. If from Dr. Newman's number of children born annually, 1,238, is subtracted first 348 who die in the first year and then 193 who die in the next five years, the remainder is 697 and not 692. The calculations of the tables of deaths, on account of their condensations and possible errors, do not demonstrate clearly the final conclusion.

82. *Postlethwayt*, I, 68, entry "Annuities."

The average of human life by these tables
appears to be about 28½, 29 - years.

o o o o o

Doctor Halley has calculated the value of lives on the following
scale

Age	Years Purchase	Age	Years Purchase	Age	Years Purchase
1	10.28	25	12.27	50	9.21
5	13.40	30	11.72	55	8.51
10	13.44	35	11.12	60	7.60
15	13.33	40	10.57	65	6.54
20	12.78	45	9.91	70	5.32[83]

It has been found by experience that the total number of the
inhabitance of the country is to the births as 35 to 1 — and in
England for a number of years the males and females born have
been as 18 to 17 — Women in every period have been observed
to live three or four years longer than men —

In England the proportion in 100,000[84] people has been estimated as follows:

Married men and women 34.500
Widowers 1.500
Unmarried youth and children 45.000
Servants 10.000
Travellers, strangers, etc. 4.000

o o o o o

Short Rule to determine the average interest per annum for any
sum of money for a given term of years at a given rate, discharg-
ing annually an equal proportion of the principle — Example

Suppose A should borrow of B 1.200.000 £ payable in twenty
years, one twentieth part or 60,000 £ annually, interest at 8 per
cent per annum, what would be the average sum each year to
pay off the whole interest in twenty years? Answer 50.400 £

83. *Ibid.*, I, 69, entry "Annuities." Also Rolt, entry "Annuities."
84. *Postlethwayt*, I, 73 gives: Servants . . . 10,500.

Process and rule

Sum borrowed . . . 1.200.000

find the amount of the interest for one year say . . . .

£96.000 —

take the mean of the number of years that is if 20 — 10½

Multiply the interest of the whole sum for one year with this mean of 10½ divide the product by 20 the number of years and the quotient will be the sum required — 50.400[85]

o o o o o

280

Quere? Would it not be advisable to let all taxes even those imposed by the states be collected by persons of Congressional appointment and would it not be advisable to pay the collectors so much per cent on the sums collected?[86]

o o o o o

Money coined in England from the Reign of Queen Elizabeth to that of George 1st inclusive that is from the year 1558 — to 1727

169 years

In Elizabeth's Reign . . .	£5,513,711	11	1¼
James 1st	5,432,351	13	9
Charles 1st	12,096,220	—	—
Charles 2d	7,899,434	2	1¼
James 2d	2,631,955	8	1 ¾

Great Recoinage
amounted to £6,435,039 14 9½

King Williams reign	10,511,963	17	11 ¾
Queen Anne's	2,691,626	6	8½
George 1st	8,725,921	15	6

| £55,503,184 | 15 | 3[87] |

---

85. This "short rule" is not included in *Postlethwayt*. It seems that Hamilton copied it from another work.

86. See Introduction p. 21.

87. *Postlethwayt*, I, 909–12, entry "Gold."

o o o o o

281

When you can get more of foreign coin for your native exchange is said to be high — and the reverse low — for instance when for a bill of one crown of three livres in France on Holland you can get 60 gross exchange is high when only fifty it is low — the par is 54 —

That is when the native money is worth more than the par in foreign, exchange is high when worth less it is low —[88]

o o o o o

America. Wool may become an article of trade. We may raise goats in the southern colonies for the skin and hair —[89]

o o o o o

282

Woad	Argol	Madder	Fuller's earth
Portugal Trade			
Ambergrease			
Biscay Spanish Trade			

Trade	*Artificers Asphaltum*		Money
Exchange	Par of Exchange		*Ballance of Trade*
	Manufacturers		Marcasite
Florence			*Talc*
Genoa			Azores
Venice	*Bullion*		*Actions*＊
Leghorn	*Assais*		Bubbles
Sicily	Standard of Gold and Silver		South Sea
Geneva	Refining		Company
Foundery	Gold Silver		Antimony†
London	Coin		Aqua Regia
Amsterdam	Merchant (Court Merchant)		Aqua fortis
Hamburgh	*Council of Trade*		Antwerp†
Paris	Naval Power		Brussels†

88. *Ibid.*, I, 742, entry "Exchange."
89. It seems that this is Hamilton's own thought.

Denmark	*Fishery*	Hamburgh
Brass*	Furr Trade Peltry	Land
Babylon	*Lapis Lazuli*	Soil
		Vegetation[90]

O   O   O   O   O

90. This is a note on various topics which Hamilton intended, perhaps, to study in *Postlethwayt*. The treatment of several of them, however, cannot be found in separate entries, but in sundry places within the *Dictionary*. The cross and asterisk signs which follow a few of the above words remain inexplicable.

III

Philosophic Premises of Hamilton's Thought

In his own lifetime Alexander Hamilton played a central role
in the controversies over policies and programs which contended
for dominance in the early, precedent-fashioning councils of the
American republic. Neither death nor time has retired Hamilton,
in the role of myth hero-villain, from the stage of controversy. He
figures so powerfully in our contemporary clash of opinion that
it is difficult to restore him to his own historical milieu, to view
him entirely unaltered by the lights and shadows cast by the con-
tentions of recent America. So long as liberals oppose conserva-
tives, the friends of capitalism reply to its critics, and similar
oppositions continue, men will be impelled to agree or disagree
with Hamilton-the-ghost rather than to seek to understand Ham-
ilton-the-man.

Even students of Hamilton have shown a regrettable tendency
to pursue controversy at the expense of historical accuracy, depth,
completeness and insight. They have helped to make "Hamiltonian" a familiar label in the exchange of ideas on problems of
which Hamilton never dreamed, while the actual content of
his thought and the context to which it applied are much neg-
lected. The current task of Hamilton scholarship is to penetrate
the legends and misconceptions nourished by controversy in
order to obtain a deeper understanding of the historic Hamilton.

The present study seeks to contribute in a small way to the fulfillment of this task.

What is attempted here is a preliminary analysis of Hamilton's thought. Such an analysis can be made through a study of his known works in order to deduce their general philosophic trends, as well as through a search of his statements in which he designedly revealed his own philosophy.

This latter task has been proven very fruitful. Misunderstandings resulting from semantic differences between eighteenth century terminology and our contemporary phrasing can be avoided to a great degree; and somewhat arbitrary conclusions, stemming primarily from the scholar's philosophic preconceptions, can be also eliminated. The student of Hamilton's works is fortunate for in explaining the process of his thought, Hamilton furnished most valuable information not only on the meaning of the terms he employed, but also on the significance he attributed to each one of them. Moreover, by frequently discussing important philosophic questions, he helped much to clarify his position in "this enlightened age."[1]

1. *"When will men learn to profit by experience?"*

Hamilton's notes in his Military Company's "Pay Book" reveal how early he developed a concern for his country's troubles, a concern that accompanied him up to the moment of his death. Some of the problems, to be sure, were quite old and their solution had been attempted by the several colonies at different times within the framework of the British imperial system. Most of the

1. "The Farmer Refuted," February 5, 1775, in Henry Cabot Lodge, ed., *The Works of Alexander Hamilton* (12 vols., 2nd ed., New York, 1904), I, 61. The material used in the writing of this part comes from the Alexander Hamilton Manuscripts, deposited in the Manuscripts Division of the Library of Congress, and from the two publications of his *Works*, the one edited by Lodge (hereafter cited as *Lodge*), and the other by John C. Hamilton, *The Works of Alexander Hamilton* (7 vols., New York, 1850), hereafter cited as *Works*. To avoid duplicate documentation, Lodge only will be cited, at the sacrifice, unfortunately, of some pertinent illustrations of Hamilton's thought.

problems, however, were new, arising from the "novelty" of their situation. After independence had been achieved, the relationship between the American community and Great Britain had changed; the political situation, having at its center the quest for an effective government, posed grave and completely new questions; the administrative problems had become more complex and the Americans were not entirely ready to deal with them. Hamilton said in retrospect:

> It would be the extreme of vanity in us not to be sensible that we began this revolution with very vague and confined notions of the practical business of government. To the greater part of us it was a novelty; of those who under the former constitution had had opportunities of acquiring experience, a large proportion adhered to the opposite side, and the remainder can only be supposed to have possessed ideas adapted to the narrow colonial sphere in which they had been accustomed to move, not of that enlarged kind suited to the government of an independent nation.[2]

Moreover, the economy, the defense, and in general the position of the feeble United States in the middle of an old and fighting world, gave the Americans new problems. A profoundly significant change was taking place. Even the old problems, in the light of the novel conditions, had become new; and they remained so for a long time during the formative period of the American nation.

Dealing with such problems, Hamilton felt the need of a guide to lead his thoughts along a safe path, to enable him to acquire necessary knowledge and to give security to his conclusions. He found such a guide in *experience*.

Hamilton thought that in many instances experience could teach or confirm the truth;[3] that "experience alone can determine

2. "The Continentalist," No. 1, July 12, 1781, *Lodge*, I, 243–44.
3. Convention of New York state, Speech on the Senate of the United States, June 25, 1788, *Lodge*, II, 53; "The Continentalist," No. 2, July 19, 1781, *Lodge*, I, 251.

with certainty the effect";[4] that "experience only can decide"[5] or that one should "let experience decide";[6] that "experience only can solve (questions) with certainty";[7] and that "experience is the parent of wisdom, . . . an adage the truth of which is recognized by the wisest as well as the simplest of mankind."[8] For him experience could "demonstrate" a situation,[9] "manifest"[10] and "exemplify"[11] a fact, "regulate" or "justify" a point of view,[12] "support and fix" an opinion,[13] "assert" an aspect,[14] "verify a theory,"[15] "prove" a thesis,[16] "convince" people,[17] "establish" maxims[18] and

4. Outline of William Smith's speech on Madison's Resolutions, January 3, 1794, draft by Hamilton, *Lodge,* IV, 215; Convention of New York, Speech on the Compromises of the Constitution, June 20, 1788, *Lodge,* II, 17.

5. Outline of Smith's Speech, *Lodge,* IV, 208.

6. "Camillus," No. 21, 1795, *Lodge,* V, 446; see also Hamilton to George Washington, October 24, 1793, *Lodge,* VIII, 112.

7. Letter No. 13 of H. G., March 7, 1789, *Lodge,* II, 161; Hamilton to George Washington (Cabinet Paper), April 1793, *Lodge,* IV, 387.

8. "Federalist," No. 72, *Lodge,* XI, 215.

9. "Defence of the Funding System" (not dated) *Lodge,* IX, 3.

10. "First Report on the Public Credit," Communicated to the House of Representatives, December 13, 1790, *Lodge,* II, 341–42.

11. "Address to the Electors of the State of New York," 1801, *Lodge,* VII, 190.

12. "Defence of the Funding System" (not dated), *Lodge,* VIII, 452.

13. "Convention of New York," June 28, 1788, *Lodge,* II, 83.

14. "Defence of the Funding System" (not dated), *Lodge,* IX, 16; Hamilton to Robert Morris, 1780, *Lodge,* III, 356.

15. "Report on the National Bank," Communicated to the House of Representatives, December 14, 1790, *Lodge,* III, 393; Letter from Phocion, No. 2, 1784, *Lodge,* IV, 289; Hamilton to George Washington, December 2, 1794, *Lodge,* X, 80.

16. "Publius," October 26, 1778, *Lodge,* I, 201; "Report on the National Bank," *Lodge,* III, 392; Camillus, No. 6, 1795, *Lodge,* V, 246.

17. "The Continentalist," No. 1, July 12, 1781, *Lodge,* I, 245.

18. "Report on Manufactures," Communicated to the House of Representatives December 5, 1791, *Lodge,* IV, 139; "Examination of Jefferson's Message to Congress of December 7, 1801" (hereafter referred to as "Jefferson's Message"), No. 16, March 19, 1802, *Lodge,* VIII, 347.

principles,[19] "show" the way,[20] "recommend" policies,[21] "lead" men to action[22] and "guide" them,[23] "confirm confidence" on a certain measure,[24] "bring" a cure to an evil,[25] "correct" conditions,[26] "teach"[27] and, most important, define knowledge.[28]

Men, according to Hamilton, could utilize any kind of experience, no matter who had undergone it, or where and when it had occurred. Thus, Hamilton very often relied on his own experience[29] or on his own experience together with that of his compatriots.[30]

Sometimes Hamilton appealed directly to the experience of

19. Speech on the Revenue System before the New York Legislature, 1787, *Lodge,* II, 204.

20. "The Continentalist," No. 5, April 18, 1782, *Lodge,* I, 272; "First Report on the Public Credit," January 14, 1790, *Lodge,* II, 274; "Operations of the Act Laying Duties on Imports," April 23, 1790, *Lodge,* II, 309; "The Public Conduct and Character of John Adams, Esq., President of the United States," 1800, *Lodge,* VII, 339.

21. "Report on the Establishment of a Mint," Communicated to the House of Representatives, January 28, 1791, *Lodge,* IV, 26.

22. "Report on the Improvement of the Revenue," Communicated to the House of Representatives, February 2, 1795, *Lodge,* III, 301; "Camillus," No. 21, 1795, *Lodge,* V, 445; Military Papers, Circular, May 23, 1799, *Lodge,* VII, 84.

23. "Report on Manufactures," *Lodge,* IV, 134; "Federalist," No. 6, *Lodge,* XI, 38.

24. "Report on Public Credit," Communicated to the Senate, January 16 and 21, 1795, *Lodge,* III, 255; "Defence of the Funding System" (not dated), *Lodge,* VIII, 464.

25. "Report on the National Bank," *Lodge,* III, 397.

26. *Lodge,* III, 403; "The Continentalist," No. 1, July 12, 1781, *Lodge,* I, 245.

27. Convention of New York, June 27, 1788, *Lodge,* II, 61; "Report on Manufactures," *Lodge,* IV, 104; "Letter from Phocion," No. 2, 1784, *Lodge,* IV, 284; "Jefferson's Message," No. 16, March 19, 1802, *Lodge,* VIII, 347.

28. "Report on the National Bank," *Lodge,* III, 420. For the significance attributed by Hamilton to experience see also Lodge, I, 225–26, 269; II, 180, 358, 385, 402, 459; III, 259, 290, 421; IV, 25, 115; V, 9, 79, 270; VI, 274, 450; VII, 95, 106, 205; VIII, 241, 443; IX, 182, 481; X, 326.

29. *Lodge,* II, 30; VII, 129, 314.

30. *Lodge,* I, 218; II, 43, 218; IV, 109; V, 80; VI, 109.

his fellow Americans,[31] and in case their experience was not sufficient, he promptly recalled the "experience of others." He indicated how important it was for him to do so, when he stated: "Self-sufficiency and a contempt of the science and experience of others are too prevailing traits of character in this country. But as far as I am to be concerned, auxiliary lights are a sine qua non."[32] This experience of "others" could be found in England, in France, in Switzerland, in Germany, in the United Provinces,[33] in the practices of "the governments of Europe,"[34] in the "experience in other countries."[35] Or Hamilton sought precedent and example in "universal experience."[36]

From the point of view of the time in which a valuable experience could occur, Hamilton believed that any experience from the past could be useful. He expressed this opinion on several occasions[37] and in this past experience he covered a span of time from a daily experience"[38] to an "experience of centuries"[39] or an "experience of past ages,"[40] "the testimony of past ages,"[41] or "the experience of all times."[42]

This is the reason why Hamilton, every time he wanted to "judge of the future by the past,"[43] resorted to history. There he

31. *Lodge,* I, 36; III, 8.

32. Hamilton to John Jay, November 19, 1798, *Lodge* VI, 487.

33. *Lodge,* I, 24, 217–18; II, 64; IV, 32.

34. "No Jacobin," 1793, *Lodge,* V, 44.

35. "Report on Public Credit," *Lodge,* III, 266; Hamilton to McHenry, November 23, 1799, *Lodge,* VII, 185.

36. Hamilton to Governor Clinton, February 24, 1793, *Lodge,* IX, 314. On the importance Hamilton attributed to the process of experiencing or to an experienced situation see also *Lodge,* I, 41; II, 149, 153, 205, 317; III, 152, 278, 302, 305, 321; IV, 20, 44, 71, 91, 96, 101, 114, 123, 248, 281, 293, 456, 468; V, 87, 247, 208, 243, 469; VI, 242, 400, 410; VII, 179.

37. *Lodge,* III, 198, 327; V, 78; VII, 35; VIII, 372; IX, 278.

38. *Lodge,* I, 331; III, 296, 389.

39. "Report on the National Bank," 1790, *Lodge,* III, 389.

40. "The Farmer Refuted," February 5, 1775, *Lodge,* I, 72.

41. *Lodge,* I, 163.

42. Hamilton to James A. Bayard, January 16, 1801, *Lodge,* X, 417.

43. "The Continentalist," No. 4, August 30, 1781, *Lodge,* I, 266.

could find all the past experience of mankind he needed, not only to enable him to fortify an argument and make his opinion convincing to others but also to guide him in forming new opinions and making further decisions.

History was commonly used by eighteenth century American thinkers for the same reasons that Hamilton resorted to it. One can safely say, however, that, with the possible exceptions of John Adams, Thomas Jefferson and James Madison, no other great man in this country during that period made so persistent and frequent use of history as did Hamilton. His conviction about its importance as the depository of human experience was repeatedly expressed. Explaining Jefferson's Message to Congress of December 7, 1801, he referred to "our histories and traditions" and added that "prudence requires us to trace the history further. . . . Perhaps a lesson is here taught which ought not to be despised."[44] The anticipation of the activities of demagogues and political opportunists was partly at least the result of his knowledge of history. Thus he maintained that "it is only to consult the history of nations, to perceive, that every country at all times, is cursed by the existence of men who, actuated by an irregular ambition, scruple nothing which they imagine will contribute to their own advancement and importance";[45] and on another occasion, he remarked that "the history of mankind is too full of these melancholy instances of human contradictions."[46] Hamilton strove to find in history facts "that can authorize" a certain statement;[47] he "appealed" to history in order to illuminate a situation;[48] and he recalled history to put a "matter out of all doubt."[49]

It was not, however, the "experience of the past" only that could be useful to men. For Hamilton equally important was the

44. "Jefferson's Message," No. 7, January 7, 1802, *Lodge*, VIII, 287.
45. "Camillus," No. 1, July 22, 1795, *Lodge*, V, 190.
46. "Letters from Phocion," No. 2, 1784, *Lodge*, IV, 268; see also Hamilton to George Washington (Cabinet Paper), April 14, 1794, *Lodge*, V, 99.
47. "No Jacobin," *Lodge*, V, 40.
48. "Convention of New York," June 21, 1788, *Lodge*, I, 442.
49. "Vindication of the Funding System," No. 3, 1791 (?), *Lodge*, III, 17.

"experience of the future." In this latter kind of experience, men could test their actions, correct, and improve them, acquire a deeper understanding of their utility and expediency, and, being able to evaluate their actions better, they could decide whether or not to continue them.

He was very explicit in his views about the "experience of the future." Speaking on the measures taken for the restoration of the public credit in Washington's first administration, he remarked with confidence that "the actual benefits or actual evils of the measures connected with the Treasury Department, present and future, would be cheerfully submitted to the TEST OF EXPERIENCE." And he accused his opponents that they "dare not trust the appeal to such a TEST."[50] Again, discussing the development of the country's manufactures and proposing the free importation of iron from abroad, Hamilton added: "The measure suggested ought, perhaps, rather to be contemplated subject to the lights of further experience, than immediately adopted."[51] Furthermore, he reserved the expansion of measures he proposed for the establishment of a mint, "till experience shall decide" on them.[52] On another occasion, explaining to Congress his measures for the organization of the National Bank and adverting to the difficulties arising from the establishment of a plurality of branches, Hamilton suggested that "the most that would seem advisable, on this point, is to insert a provision which may lead to it hereafter, if experience shall more clearly demonstrate its utility and satisfy those who may have the direction, that it may be adopted with safety."[53] Talking also about the proposed removal of certain officers active during the Whiskey Rebellion, he stated to George Washington that "experience, however, may better explain in a little time, whether any concession on that point will

50. "Civis to Mercator," No. 2, September 11, 1792, *Lodge,* III, 39.
51. "Report on Manufactures," *Lodge,* IV, 169.
52. "Report on the Establishment of a Mint," *Lodge,* IV, 48.
53. "Report on the National Bank," *Lodge,* III, 425.

be expedient";[54] and on the same occasion, supporting the advisability of forebearance in urging coercive measures, he added: "till further time for reflection and experience of its operation had served to correct false impressions and inspire greater moderation."[55] Again, writing to Colonel Edward Carrington on the reports he had concerning the unfriendliness of James Madison, Hamilton asserted that he had resolved to overlook these reports and wait "till time and more experience should afford a solution" to the problem arising from his former colleague's attitude.[56] In the same letter Hamilton made the following interesting statement about republicanism:

> I said I was affectionately attached to the republican theory. This is the real language of my heart, which I open to you in the sincerity of friendship; and I add that I have strong hopes of the success of that theory; but, in candor, I ought also to add that I am far from being without doubts. I consider its success as yet a problem. It is yet to be determined by experience whether it be consistent with that stability and order in government which are essential to public strength and private security and happiness.[57]

In many other instances, Hamilton expressed his deep respect for the "experience of the future."[58]

In general, his writings pay an almost exaggerated homage to the value of experience. He preferred to use "experience, sad experience,"[59] or "bitter experience"[60] rather than to find himself helpless, "untaught by . . . experience."[61] He expressed his indig-

54. Hamilton to George Washington, June 4, 1794, *Lodge*, VI, 350.

55. *Lodge*, VI, 364.

56. Hamilton to Carrington, May 26, 1792, *Lodge*, IX, 517.

57. *Lodge*, IX, 534.

58. See *Lodge*, II, 28, 280, 325, 346, 447; III, 380; V, 234; VII, 186; VIII, 260; IX, 447, 451, 454.

59. "Jefferson's Message," No. 12, February 23, 1802, *Lodge*, VIII, 322.

60. Speech on the Revenue System before the New York Legislature, 1787, *Lodge*, II, 204.

61. "The Stand," No. 6, April 19, 1798, *Lodge*, VI, 305.

nation against those who were more "fond of hypothesis than experience,"[62] and he exclaimed with wrath: "When will men learn to profit by experience?"[63]

2. "Reason and Experience teach us."

In considering the omnipotent role attributed by Hamilton to experience, one is tempted to classify him among the most ardent empiricists. A careful study of Hamilton's works, however, reveals that for him it was not only experience but also reason that defined knowledge. Hamilton expressed this concept on several occasions. Speaking about the Federal Government's obligation to provide the means for the common defense of the country, although he primarily relied on experience, he nevertheless stated:

> Reason and experience teach that the great mass of expense in every country proceeds from war. Our experience has already belied the reveries of those dreamers or impostors who were wont to weaken the argument arising from this source by promising to this country a perpetual exemption from war.[64]

Again, on the eve of the Revolution, when discussing the measures taken by the colonies and their consequences for Great Britain, although basically he relied on experience, he acknowledged reason as well:

> Reason and experience teach us that the consequences would be too fatal to Great Britain to admit of delay. There is an immense trade between her and the colonies. The revenues arising from thence are prodigious. The consumption of her manufactures in these colonies supplies the means of subsistence to a vast number of her most useful inhabitants. The experiment we have made heretofore shows us of how much importance our commercial connection is to her, and gives us the

62. "Catullus," No. 3, September 29, 1792, *Lodge*, VII, 272.

63. Hamilton to Harrison Gray Otis, January 26, 1799, *Lodge*, X, 339.

64. "Defence of the Funding System," II (written probably after 1795), *Lodge*, IX, 6.

highest assurance of obtaining immediate redress by suspending it.[65]

Writing, also, to John Jay on the expediency of raising a few battalions of Negroes in the southern states during the Revolution, he remarked that: "The contempt we have been taught to entertain for the blacks, makes us fancy many things that are founded neither in reason nor experience."[66] When he explained to George Washington the measures to be taken during the Whiskey Rebellion, he asserted:

> The idea of giving time for the law to extend itself in scenes where the dissatisfaction with it was the effect not of an improper spirit, but of causes which were of a nature to yield to reason, reflection, and experience (which had constantly weighed in the estimate of the measures proper to be pursued), had had its effect in an extensive degree. The experiment, too, had been long enough tried to ascertain, that where resistance continued, the root of the evil lay deep, and required measures of greater efficacy than had been pursued.[67]

In proposing his plan for the establishment of a mint, he stated: "As far as relates to the tendency of a free coinage to produce an increase of expense in the different ways that have been stated, the argument must be allowed to have foundation both in reason and in experience. It described what has been exemplified in Great Britain."[68]

In most of these cases where Hamilton recalls both experience and reason in order to derive or ascertain the truth of a statement, there is more weight accorded to experience than to reason. Yet the appeal to reason is there, almost side by side with the

65. "A Full Vindication," *Lodge*, I, 16–17.
66. Hamilton to John Jay, Headquarters, March 14, 1779, *Lodge*, IX, 161.
67. Hamilton to George Washington, Treasury Department, August 5, 1794, *Lodge*, VI, 381.
68. "Report on the Establishment of a Mint," *Lodge*, IV, 31.

appeal to experience. This is neither contradictory nor surprising. Hamilton belonged to the "modern" minds who, appearing after the time of Isaac Newton, always employed both experience and reason in order to arrive at safe conclusions. The question, consequently, does not appear to be why Hamilton, apparently an empiricist, appealed also to reason, but rather what he meant by reason and how he employed it in relation to experience.

3. *"The voice of nature and reason."*

A close study of all known cases in which Hamilton referred to reason shows that he employed it with two main connotations. According to the first, reason is a quality, filling the universe, and revealing itself in human minds. According to the second, reason is a function of a faculty with which man is endowed and which follows or should follow certain rules, the rules of logic, a process that leads to safe conclusions.

Reason as a universal quality, implying a divine authority, discoverable and comprehensible, was the well-established concept of the Enlightenment and constituted the fundamental premise of the so-called Natural Rights philosophy in which Hamilton had been schooled. By referring to it, he was merely repeating the ideas of the vast majority of contemporary thinkers. In this connotation he employed reason mostly in a general, abstract manner, often coupled with the word "nature," which manifested reason's catholic, universal and uniform value. It was in this sense that Hamilton asserted: "all which I have by general arguments proved are constant to reason and nature."[69] In like manner he concluded a series of arguments by maintaining: "This is the conclusion of nature and reason."[70] With this meaning, when condemning violation of faith in international relations, he asked: "What sentence would natural reason, unwarped by particular dogmas, pronounce on such a conduct?"[71]

69. "The Farmer Refuted," *Lodge,* I, 136.
70. "Pacificus," No. 5, July 13, 1792, *Lodge,* IV, 473.
71. "Camillus," No. 19, 1795, *Lodge,* V, 416.

It was in the same sense, so familar to the eighteenth century *philosophes*, that Hamilton on other occasions made statements such as: "Reason, religion, philosophy, policy, disavow the spurious and odious doctrine, that we ought to cherish and cultivate enmity with any nation whatever."[72] "It is a plain dictate of reason and an established principle of the law of nations that a neutral state in any matter relating to war . . . cannot lawfully succor, aid, countenance, or support either of the parties at war with each other."[73]

It is interesting to note, however, that in most instances in which Hamilton employed "the voice of reason"[74] or "the voice of nature,"[75] in the connotation given by the Natural Rights philosophy, he referred to two subjects: first, to the causes that made the Americans fight their Revolution; and second, to the laws that should define international relations. In a sense, the subjects are related.

His thoughts on this matter were very clear and in perfect agreement with the philosophy of the Enlightenment. He maintained that the laws of nations were founded upon "the principles of reason and natural justice."[76] These were clearly a manifestation of natural law, which was thus described:

> . . . the Deity, from the relations we stand in to Himself and to each other, has constituted an eternal and immutable law, which is indispensably obligatory upon all mankind, prior to any human institution whatever. This is what is called the law of nature.[77]

And quoting Blackstone on this subject, Hamilton explained that

72. "Horatius," May, 1795, *Lodge,* V, 184.
73. "No Jacobin," No. 4, 1793, *Lodge,* V, 40–41. Also, *Lodge,* VI, 307. For similar uses of reason see, also *Lodge,* III, 357; IV, 6, 321, 375, 377; V, 95–96, 195, 197, 374; VI, 228; VIII, 226, 434.
74. Hamilton to George Washington (Cabinet Paper), Philadelphia, April 14, 1794, *Lodge,* V, 100.
75. "The Farmer Refuted," *Lodge,* I, 114.
76. "Camillus," No. 33, 1796, *Lodge,* VI, 130–31.
77. "A Full Vindication," *Lodge,* I, 62.

natural law, being coeval with mankind and dictated by God himself, was superior in obligations to any other. It was binding over all the globe, in all countries, and at all times. No human laws were of any validity, if contrary to this; and such of them as were valid derived all their authority, mediately or immediately, from the original. Upon this law depended the natural rights of mankind.[78]

Hamilton's belief in the above premises was manifested on many occasions. His notion of the divine origin of natural rights could not be better reflected than in this positive statement:

THE SACRED RIGHTS OF MANKIND ARE NOT TO BE RUMMAGED FOR AMONG OLD PARCHMENTS OR MUSTY RECORDS. THEY ARE WRITTEN, AS WITH A SUNBEAM, IN THE WHOLE VOLUME OF HUMAN NATURE, BY THE HAND OF THE DIVINITY ITSELF AND CAN NEVER BE ERASED OR OBSCURED BY MORTAL POWER.[79]

The superiority of natural law, its quality as an infallible standard with reference to which men were able to judge their own laws is evident in statements like the following:

When the first principles of civil society are violated, and the rights of a whole people are invaded, the common forms of municipal law are not to be regarded. Men may then betake themselves to the law of nature; and, if they but conform their actions to that standard, all cavils against them betray either ignorance or dishonesty.[80]

He disapproved of the excesses and extravagances of the French Revolution "from which reason and humanity recoil."[81] He approved, however, of the clause included in the Jay Treaty providing for non-confiscation of enemy property, because the provision was "so just and perspicuous as to speak conviction to the heart

78. *Lodge,* I, 62–63.
79. "The Farmer Refuted," *Lodge,* I, 113. Hamilton's emphasis.
80. *Lodge,* I, 135.
81. "Americanus," February 1, 1794, *Lodge,* V, 76.

and understanding, (it) unites the natural with the customary law of nations."[82] He declared the sanctity of those points of the common law when he found that they were "Natural law and natural reason applied to the purposes of society."[83] Discussing again the Jay Treaty, he asserted:

> Yes, in controversies between nations, respecting the application of the rules of the laws of nations, decisions of the highest court of one of the parties, if contrary to these rules, are illegal. In other words, they are contrary to that law, which is the standard of legality between nations.[84]

On the other hand, Hamilton's references to common-sense stressed his belief in the universal acceptance of natural law and in the uniformity of its appeal to all men. In an early period, he had maintained that the enemies of the Revolution had

> an invincible aversion to common-sense (which) is apparent in many respects: they endeavor to persuade us that the absolute sovereignty of Parliament does not imply our absolute slavery; that it is a Christian duty to submit to be plundered of all we have; . . . that slavery, so far from being a great evil, is a great blessing; and even that our contest with Britain is founded entirely upon the petty duty of three pence per pound on East India tea, whereas the whole world knows it is built upon this interesting question, whether the inhabitants of Great Britain have a right to dispose of the lives and properties of the inhabitants of America, or not.[85]

In a later period, Hamilton denied the right of the Legislature to disfranchise any number of citizens by general proscription and to deprive them of hearing or trial, because then "the name of liberty applied to such a government would be a mockery of com-

82. "Camillus," No. 21, 1795, *Lodge,* V, 443.
83. Speech in the case of Harry Croswell, 1804, *Lodge,* VIII, 421.
84. Hamilton to Oliver Wolcott, New York, October 3, 1795, *Lodge,* X, 117–18.
85. "A Full Vindication," *Lodge,* I, 4–5.

mon-sense."[86] He rejected the possibility that state governments might become the oppressors of the people and might combine to destroy the liberties and happiness of their fellow citizens, and he protested against such an attitude: "The idea is shocking! It outrages every feeling of humanity, and every dictate of common-sense!"[87] In his words: "Sir, we cannot reason from probabilities alone. When we leave common-sense, and give ourselves up to conjectures, there can be no certainty, no security in our reasonings."[88]

While these references to "the general sense of mankind"[89] occurred frequently,[90] the following statement in which Hamilton discussed the delicate question of how a law of nations, which is a manifestation of natural law, could be changed, clearly indicates his concept of man's uniform and general acceptance of natural law as expressed by the *consensus universalis:*

A pre-established rule of the law of nations can only be changed by their *common consent.* This consent may either be express, by treaties, declarations, etc., adopting and promising the observance of a different rule, or it may be implied by a course of practice or usage. The consent, in either case, must embrace the great community of civilized nations. If to be inferred from treaties, it must be shown that they are uniform and universal. It can, at least, never be inferred, while the treaties of different nations follow different rules, or the treaties between the same nation and other vary from each other. So also as to usage. It must be uniform and universal, and, let it be added, it must be continued. A usage adopted by some nations, and resisted by others, or adopted by all temporarily and then discontinued, is insufficient to abolish an old, or substitute a new rule of the law of nations.[91]

86. Convention of New York, June 27, 1788, *Lodge,* II, 70.
87. *Lodge,* II, 72–73; see also *Lodge,* I, 76–77.
88. Convention of New York, *Lodge,* II, 72–73.
89. "Letters from Phocion, No. 2," 1784, *Lodge,* IV, 255.
90. See also *Lodge,* I, 171, 269; IV, 400; V, 41.
91. "Camillus," No. 31, 1795, *Lodge,* VI, 100; On the same topic see *Lodge,* V, 200, 474; VI, 113.

Besides Hamilton's explicit statements concerning his concept of Natural Rights, his own phraseology often betrays the impact of this philosophy on him. He frequently used expressions so familiar among the thinkers of his times, such as "common nature,"[92] "human nature,"[93] "real nature,"[94] "the nature of the thing,"[95] "state of nature,"[96] "natural source of things,"[97] "common right,"[98] "natural rights of mankind,"[99] "freedom of opinion of mankind,"[100] "inalienable rights of mankind,"[101] "principles of humanity,"[102] "enlightened reason,"[103] "natural justice,"[104] "natural liberty,"[105] "principles of universal liberty,"[106] and so on.

Hamilton's reliance on Natural Rights can easily be explained. During the period of the American Revolution, when specific issues and grievances were raised to the heights of universal values; and a little later, when the infant nation of the United States

92. "A Full Vindication," *Lodge,* I, 6.

93. "Address to the Independent and Patriotic Electors of the State of New York, March, 1789," *Lodge,* II, 122; "Vindication of the Funding System," No. 1, 1791, *Lodge,* III, 6; "Letters from Phocion," No. 2, 1784, *Lodge,* IV, 290; "The Warning," No. 1, January 27, 1797, *Lodge,* VI, 234.

94. Hamilton to George Washington, May 2, 1793, *Lodge,* IV, 404; France, 1796, *Lodge,* VI, 208.

95. "Camillus," No. 6, 1795, *Lodge,* V, 247; Defence of the Funding System, No. 2 (not dated), *Lodge,* IX, 3; also, Report on Manufactures, *Lodge,* IV, 126.

96. "Report on Public Credit," *Lodge,* III, 291, 293.

97. "Camillus," No. 10, 1795, *Lodge,* V, 290.

98. "A Full Vindication," *Lodge,* I, 6.

99. *Lodge,* 63; "Camillus," No. 20, 1795, *Lodge,* V, 431, 442.

100. Hamilton to George Washington, May 2, 1793, *Lodge,* IV, 405.

101. Convention of New York, June 28, 1788, *Lodge,* II, 78.

102. "Camillus," *No.* 2, 1795, *Lodge,* V, 200, 237; "Americanus," No. 1, February 1, 1794, *Lodge,* V, 76.

103. "Report on Public Credit," January 16, 1795, *Lodge,* III, 291, 293. Hamilton's favorite expression of "enlightened" occurred in various relationships, such as "enlightened people" (*Lodge,* V, 234), "enlightened opponents" (*Lodge,* III, 361), "enlightened nation" (*Lodge,* III, 389; IV, 284).

104. "A Full Vindication," *Lodge,* I, 6; "Camillus," No. 33, 1796, *Lodge,* VI, 130.

105. *Lodge,* VI, 130.

106. "Letters from Phocion," No. 1, 1784, *Lodge,* IV, 234.

found itself in the midst of a hostile world and the question of fundamental principles to guide its relations with the various countries appeared with intense acuteness, no other system of thought could better express the issues involved than Natural Rights philosophy.

Moreover, most situations where Hamilton resorted to the philosophy of Natural Rights were related to what can be called principles of international law. In doing so, Hamilton quoted, often without any acknowledgement some of the greatest masters in this field, such as Grotius, Vattel, Puffendorf, Blackstone, Burlemaqui, Bynkershoek, Jenkins, Valin and others.[107] These men were not only the most important founders of international law, but were also among the greatest expounders of Natural Rights, on which they exclusively based their theories. Thus Hamilton, relying on the works of these thinkers in the field of international law, was, in a manner, obliged to use the philosophy of Natural Rights.

International law and the rights of the revolting Americans were not, however, the only areas that attracted Hamilton's intellectual activity during his lifetime. In many other instances, Hamilton employed reason in a different sense, namely, as a function of a faculty with which man is endowed.

4. *"The manner of thinking and reasoning."*

Quite early Hamilton stated: "The Supreme Being gave existence to man, together with the means of preserving and beautifying that existence. He endowed him with rational faculties, by the help of which to discern and pursue such things as were consistent with his duty and interest."[108]

Hamilton, however, did not conceive of these "rational faculties" with which the Creator endowed human beings, as a static Lydian stone testing the validity and revealing the very essence of things. Rather his notion of the faculty implied a function and made Hamilton conceive of reason, in this second connotation,

107. See, for example, *Lodge,* I, 61–64; V, 41, 426, 430–31, 442–43.
108. "A Full Vindication," *Lodge,* I, 63.

as a kind of force, an energy, as a dynamic process "by the help of which (he could) discern and pursue." It is mostly in this sense that he used reason.

This process should take place according to certain "rules of reasoning,"[109] which, if they were properly followed, could lead to the determination of truth. This kind of reasoning was called by Hamilton "fair reasoning,"[110] or "true reasoning,"[111] or "just reasoning"[112] or "good reasoning,"[113] a reasoning that was "perspicuous and convincing,"[114] and which possessed "much force."[115]

This manner of reasoning, on the basis of certain rules, was the only one that could be used to draw valid inferences, to reach safe conclusions. Reasoning, which reached different conclusions, was in error, and was termed inconclusive,[116] fallacious,[117] erroneous[118] artificial.[119]

109. Hamilton to George Washington (Cabinet Paper), July 9, 1795, *Lodge,* V, 142.

110. "Letters from Phocion," No. 1, 1784, *Lodge,* IV, 235; Hamilton to George Washington, July 9, 1795, *Lodge,* V, 151; Speech in the case of Harry Croswell, 1804, *Lodge,* VIII, 404.

111. Hamilton to Robert Morris, 1780, *Lodge,* III, 327; Hamilton to George Washington (Cabinet Papers), April, 1793, *Lodge,* IV, 385.

112. Convention of New York, June 28, 1788, *Lodge,* II, 84; "Report on Loans," Communicated to the House of Representatives, February 20, 1793, *Lodge,* III, 160; Jefferson's Message, No. 14, March 2, 1802, *Lodge,* VIII, 337.

113. "The Farmer Refuted," *Lodge,* I, 134; "Opinion as to the Constitutionality of the Bank of the United States," February 23, 1791, *Lodge,* III, 461.

114. Hamilton to George Washington (Cabinet Paper), September 15, 1790, *Lodge,* IV, 321.

115. Hamilton to Rufus King, June 15, 1793, *Lodge,* X, 47; Report on Public Credit, *Lodge,* II, 252.

116. Hamilton to John Adams, Philadelphia, August 16, 1792, *Lodge,* X, 16.

117. "Report on the Establishment of a Mint," *Lodge,* IV, 37.

118. "Americanus," No. 2, February 8, 1794, *Lodge,* V, 94.

119. "Jefferson's Message," No. 12, February 23, 1802, *Lodge,* VIII, 315.

Thus, for Hamilton, reason in this sense was not the absolute quality that was derived from, constituted a part of, and revealed the Divine design; it was an original intellectual power, a function, it was the "reasoning" of a human faculty.[120] And it seemed that often Hamilton conceived of this reasoning as synonymous with "thinking." For instance when he stated, speaking on the constitutionality of the Bank of the United States: "A strange fallacy seems to have crept into the manner of thinking and reasoning upon this subject;"[121] or when he said, defending the Jay Treaty: "I do justice to Mr. Jay's reasoning on this subject. He thought rightly that. . . ."[122] It had to be, of course, a right or logical thinking, in other words, according to the rules of logic, in order to be identified with "good reasoning." This relationship between logical and good reasoning also becomes evident in the terms related to reason, as used by Hamilton. Thus the term "reasonable," which for Hamilton was the outcome of good reasoning, was almost identical with "logical" while "unreasonable," the outcome of erroneous reasoning, could be safely replaced by the term "illogical."[123]

120. On the use of the term "reasoning" by Hamilton see also *Lodge*, I, 76; II, 33, 44, 52, 84, 86, 121, 181, 197; III, 97, 178, 304, 324, 325, 442, 452, 454, 465, 480; IV, 37, 68, 119, 121, 329; V, 217; VI, 132, 173, 180, 234; VII, 205, 223; VIII, 267; IX, 433; X, 210.

121. Hamilton to George Washington, February 23, 1791, *Lodge*, III, 451.

122. Hamilton to George Washington (Cabinet Paper), July 9, 1795, *Lodge*, V, 163.

123. A study of all relative terms in Hamilton's usage illuminates better his concept of reason as a function of a human faculty. For example, for the use of the term "reasonable" see *Lodge*, I, 9, 25, 133, 190, 395; II, 60, 250, 325, 368, 394, 413, 418; III, 150, 261, 270, 300, 302, 346, 355, 358, 384, 393, 423, 435; IV, 73, 130, 171, 239, 319, 325, 339, 375; V, 11, 144, 150, 154, 155, 163, 173, 198, 203, 208, 212, 233, 276, 302, 366, 417; VI, 271, 295, 299; VII, 4, 32, 153, 218; VIII, 46, 51, 59, 72, 93, 238, 255, 267, 463, 469; IX, 488; X, 4, 94, 143, 162, 223. For the use of the term "unreasonable" see *Lodge*, II, 45, 356, 425; IV, 72, 116, 129; V, 174, 179, 190; VI, 176, 294, 361; VII, 9. For "reasonably" *Lodge*, II, 346, 473; III, 29, 35, 258,

Since Hamilton attributed such importance to the function of reason, its further clarification becomes necessary. This can be accomplished by following Hamilton's intellectual process that aimed at the solution of his problems.

5. *The reasoning should be supported by the fact.*

Generally speaking, Hamilton's first step in solving a problem was the exhaustive collection of the empirical facts relating to a question under consideration. He systematically avoided starting from *a priori* ideas, vague and abstract notions. He wanted to be as close as possible to factual reality, and for this reason he often resorted to experience. He repeatedly expressed his distrust of those who disregarded the outcome of experience; and he frequently tested statements on the basis of facts, practice and reality. He disregarded criticism against the government that came from "some men, who constantly substitute hypothesis to fact, imagination to evidence."[124] When he discussed the revenue system in the New York Convention for the ratification of the Constitution, he argued: "I appeal to the gentleman. Have the states who suffered least contributed most? No, sir; the fact is directly the reverse. This consideration is sufficient entirely to refute the gentleman's reasoning."[125] Always striving to found his reasonings on conclusive facts, he put aside the objection of his opponents in 1798 maintaining that the issuance of ten million dollars worth of paper money in the form of bank bills would cause the banishment of the country's coin, with the simple retort: "This is

265; IV, 58, 153, 178, 183, 414; V, 85, 162, 165, 176, 227, 239, 252; VI, 344, 366, 404; VII, 220; VIII 100; IX, 540. For "unreasonably," *Lodge*, V, 51, 238. For "reasonableness," *Lodge*, IV, 338; V, 275, 378; VI, 421; IX, 312. For "unreasonableness," *Lodge*, I, 375; V, 394; VI, 311. For the term "rational," used by Hamilton in both connotations, that is, as derived from and pertaining to reason, the latter taken as an eternal verity, and also, as the outcome of "good reasoning," see *Lodge*, II, 64, 445; IV, 265; V, 213, 236, 260; VI, 425; VIII, 43; IX, 160.

124. Objections and Answers Respecting the Administration of the Government, August 18, 1792, *Lodge*, II, 466. See also *Lodge*, II, 84.

125. *Lodge*, II, 83.

a mere hypothesis, in which theorists differ. There are no decisive facts on which to rest the question."[126]

When he could demonstrate the facts on which his statement was based he felt confident and bold. Such was the case when, after he had enumerated the blessings coming from his funding system he stated: "We make these assertions boldly, because the fact is exemplified by experience, and it is obvious to all discerning men. Our opponents in their hearts know it to be so."[127] Sometimes, even in matters concerning the law of nations, he felt uncomfortable when principles of reason and natural justice were not demonstrated by facts. In a similar case, discussing Jay's Treaty, he stated:

> If we call to our aid the principles of reason and natural justice, which are the great foundations of the law of nations, we shall not discover, in this instance, *data* as certain as could be wished, for a satisfactory conclusion; and the soundest determination which we can adopt will be, that beyond a certain point, the question is in a great degree arbitrary, and must depend materially upon conventional regulation between nation and nation.[128]

Thus, this first stage of Hamilton's intellectual activity was characterized by a collection of the available empirical data, of the facts which constituted the foundation and the raw material on which his reason was to work. Then followed an inquiry into the origin of the facts, an examination of their genesis, and through observation and distinction, through comparison and combination, through the establishment of differences and relationships, an analysis as thorough as possible took place, which constituted, at the same time, the first step that led to a higher

126. "Objections and Answers Respecting the Administration of the Government," August 18, 1792, *Lodge*, II, 449. See also VIII, 112.

127. "Address to the Electors of the State of New York," 1801, *Lodge*, VII, 190, and VIII, 235.

128. "Camillus," No. 33, 1796, *Lodge*, VI, 130.

stage. Hamilton was not satisfied merely with a collection of empirical data and their detailed analysis. What he most desired was to find their deeper meaning and to establish the bond uniting these diversified facts. He achieved this through their reconstruction and synthesis. From these he derived either a conclusion with an enforced authority, or, what he really sought to establish, a principle.

One example will be enough to illustrate this process. In his letter to Robert Morris of April 30, 1781, Hamilton was confronted by the crucial problem of estimating the country's capacity for revenue and the proportion between what it was able to afford, and what it stood in need of, for the expenses of its civil and military establishments. The first step he took in order to reach a solution was the collection of empirical data related to the problem. He found these data abroad because, as he explained:

> . . . our own experience of our faculties in this respect has not been sufficiently clear or uniform, to admit of a certain conclusion; so that it will be more satisfactory to judge of them by a general principle, drawn by the example of other nations, compared with what we have effected ourselves, than to rely entirely upon the latter.[129]

From all nations he selected for his analysis three: "The nations with whose wealth and revenues we are best acquainted, are France, Great Britain and the United Provinces." Then he proceeded to a lengthy discussion of the revenue policy of these countries in relation to their wealth. He offered his own estimates, he quoted authorities such as David Hume and Dr. Richard Price, he established differences between the fiscal practices of the United Provinces and the other two countries and, passing to the stage of the reconstruction of these data, he endeavored through a comparison to detect what was common in them, to determine a rule uniting them:

129. *Lodge*, III, 345.

From these three examples we may venture to deduce this general rule, — that the proportion of revenue which a nation is capable of affording, is about one fourth of its circulating cash, so far as this is a just representative of its labor and commodities.[130]

Having reached to this "general rule," he made it clear that its application was limited. "This is only applicable to commercial countries,"[131] he stated and he explained the reasons why. Then before examining the American experience as against the conclusion from the experience abroad, he again emphasized the limited authority of the "general rule" which he had just reached:

When I say that one fourth part of its stock of wealth is the revenue which a nation is capable of affording to the government, I must be understood in a qualified, not in an absolute, sense.[132]

He elaborated more on the qualification of this "general rule," which was the result of a synthetic process on his data, and finally he found that, limited in its applications as it was, this rule could be useful for the solution of the problem under examination: "This suffices" he stated, "for a standard to us; and we may proceed to the application."[133]

6. *"Experience confirms the truth of principles."*

The "principle" which Hamilton endeavored to establish, or the "maxim," as he usually called it, was not an eternal verity of final and absolute value that would have a universal and uniform appeal to all men of all times. It was instead, the product of a rational process, a conclusion of reason's function, achieved through the analysis and synthesis of collected empirical data confined to a limited area.

Therefore, "reason" and "principle" naturally appear hand in

130. *Lodge,* III, 347.
131. *Lodge,* III, 348.
132. *Ibid.*
133. *Ibid.*

hand in Hamilton's statements. He simply indicated the process and the outcome simultaneously. He asserted, for example: "In all but direct taxes the Constitution enjoins *uniformity*. Reason and principle enjoin it with respect to all taxes laid by the same government upon the same society."[134] Or, he endeavored to prove "the right to confiscate or sequestrate private debts or private property in public funds, on the ground of reason and principle."[135]

Hamilton believed, as he asserted, that reason was the touchstone of maxims.[136] However, the validity of such a maxim or principle and its provisional extension, that is, the broadness of its authority, depended to a great degree on experience—on the facts used as raw material. The reasoning could have been "just" and "good," but nevertheless this reasoning constituted nothing more than the analysis and synthesis of empirical facts. If those facts were insufficient or improper in the first place, then the function of reason could not lead to "sound" principles. If they were lacking entirely, then the reasoning was abstract and was often discounted by Hamilton.

Hamilton repeatedly expressed his distrust of reasoning not based upon facts; for example when he discussed the defects of a confederacy he maintained that each member of a political confederacy was more disposed to advance its own authority upon the ruins of the authority of the confederacy. This respect for facts was evident when he maintained that the subjects of each member would be more devoted in their attachments and obedience to their own particular governments, than to that union:

Experience confirms the truth of these principles. The chief cities of Greece had once their council of Amphyctions, or states-general, with authority to decide and compose the differences of the several cities, and to transact many other im-

134. "Defence of the Funding System," II (not dated), *Lodge*, IX, 8. Hamilton's emphasis.
135. "Camillus," No. 19, 1795, *Lodge*, V, 413. Also in *Lodge*, IV, 375; VI, 133–34.
136. *Lodge*, IV, 377.

portant matters relative to the common interest and safety. At their first institution, they had . . .[137]

and he continued with a long list of facts taken not only from the experience of ancient Greece, but also from the German Diet, Helvetic League and the United Provinces. When again, in the New York Convention he asserted that the system of requisitions, as a revenue system, was inadequate, he reminded the Convention that the system

> depends on principles of human nature that are as infallible as any mathematical calculations. States will contribute, or not, according to their circumstances or interests. They will all be inclined to throw off their burdens of government upon their neighbors. These positions have been so fully illustrated and proved in former stages of this debate, that nothing need be added. Unanswerable experience — stubborn facts have supported and fixed them.[138]

The facts on which a principle was founded did not constitute the only circumstance determining the principle's validity. However, before examining this matter further, a parenthesis is needed to clarify Hamilton's position among the thinkers of his time. This clarification, in turn, will better illuminate the problem of the qualities of a principle as conceived by Hamilton.[139]

7. *The "Incorrigible theorists."*

To a great extent, Hamilton's mind functioned in a typical eighteenth century manner. The collection of empirical data, their analysis and reconstruction, and the arrival at conclusions of a relative and not absolute authority, comprised the process followed by the great majority of thinkers during this Age of

137. "The Continentalist," No. 2, July 19, 1781, *Lodge,* I, 251.

138. Convention of New York, June 28, 1788, *Lodge,* II, 83. See also, *Lodge,* III, 345; IV, 139; VIII, 347.

139. The discussion on the factors which, according to Hamilton, defined the validity of a principle is continued after the following subtitle No. 7.

Enlightenment. Perhaps one could say that this very process distinguished them from thinkers of previous ages.

There are, however, certain aspects of Hamilton's thinking which made him quite different from many of his contemporaries. These aspects arise from the fact that Hamilton was a man of affairs. He did not belong to those theorists who speculated for theory's sake. All his thoughts were concerned with concrete questions related most often to the economic, social and political life of the newly emerged United States. In this life Hamilton was not only a participant, but one of the protagonists. Dealing with these concrete and "practical" problems he felt a responsibility for their solution. "Abstract theoretic propositions"[140] were not for him, and his antipathy toward "theorists" detached from realities, or "theories" in disagreement with "practice," is evident in many of his statements. Thus, in his Report on Loans, attacking the "incorrigible theorists," he maintained:

> No man, placed in the office of the Secretary of the Treasury, whatever theoretic doubts he may have brought into it, would be a single month without surrendering those doubts to a full conviction, that banks are essential to the pecuniary operations of the Government.[141]

He further asserted that "No man, having a practical knowledge of the probable resources of the country. . . . No man, practically acquainted with the pecuniary ability of individuals, in this country" would disagree with him.[142]

Speaking on the funding system again he stated:

> *The public credit has been effectually restored.* This may be in the eyes of Mercator of little moment. There are certain

140. "Camillus," No. 4, 1795, *Lodge,* V, 226; also, Hamilton to George Washington (Cabinet Paper), April 1793, *Lodge,* IV, 379.

141. "Report on Loans," *Lodge,* III, 167.

142. *Ibid.* The same argument was earlier expressed in "Objections and Answers Respecting the Administration of the Government," August 18, 1792, *Lodge,* II, 459. See also *Lodge,* VIII, 50, 460.

theorists who hold both private and public credit to be pernicious. But their disciples are not numerous; at least among sober and enlightened men. The actual benefits or actual evils of the measures connected with the Treasury Department, present and future, would be cheerfully submitted to the TEST OF EXPERIENCE. Happy would it be for the country, honorable for human nature, if the experiment were permitted to be fairly made.[143]

Hamilton was happy when he could establish an agreement between theory and practice, theorists and men of practice. He was pleased, indeed, when he could speak as he did at the Constitutional Convention in Philadelphia:

All the passions, then, we see, of avarice, ambition, interest, which govern most individuals and all public bodies, fall into the current of the states, and do not flow into the stream of the General Government. The former, therefore, will generally be an overmatch for the General Government, and render any Confederacy in its very nature precarious. Theory is in this case fully confirmed by experience. The Amphictyonic Council had . . .[144]

He was glad too, when, after he had indicated that the President was the sole authority in the United States government who could constitutionally issue a declaration of neutrality, he could add: "This view of the subject is so natural and obvious, so analogous to general theory and practice, that no doubt can be entertained of its justness, unless to be deduced from particular provisions of the Constitution of the United States."[145]

8. *"There can be no doubt on a question where justice and expediency point."*

143. "Civis to Mercator," No. 2, September 11, 1792, *Lodge,* III, 39. Hamilton's emphasis.
144. Speech in the Federal Convention, Monday, June 18, 1787, *Lodge,* I, 384–85.
145. "Pacificus," No. 1, June 29, 1793, *Lodge,* IV, 437. See also *Lodge,* II, 453; III, 389.

Distrusting "abstract theories," Hamilton was almost always stimulated in his thinking by a very concrete question, a very "practical" problem. Once confronted by such a question, he conceived of it as an individual "case"; in fact, he treated it as a separate "case," even if it was similar to another one. From there on, Hamilton's objective was not only to reach a logical conclusion, but also to define the "expediency" of the practical application of the conclusion. Furthermore, if he were to proceed with the enactment of his conclusion, his goal was to define the most "expedient" measures to be taken.

Indeed, one may accurately maintain that in all the known writings of Alexander Hamilton, there is no term so frequently repeated, as the term "expediency" or "expedient." It customarily appears as soon as he had reached the point of applying in practice the outcome of his reasoning. And this persistent inquiry into the "expediency" of the conclusion in an individual case is one of the elements that made him different from so many of his contemporaries. A few examples should suffice to clarify the role dramatized by "expediency" in the process of his thought.

In April of 1790, for example, Hamilton laid before Congress his entire reasoning in making permissible the payment of duties in bank notes, instead of only in silver and gold; then he added: "Such were the reflections of the Secretary with regard to the authority to permit bank notes to be taken in payment of the duties. The expediency of doing it appeared to him to be still less questionable." And he proceeded with an analysis of the situation in order to prove the "expediency" of such a measure.[146]

Another time, in February 1787, the New York Assembly discussed the introduction of an amendment by which all British adherents who had been engaged in privateering in war should be excluded from the political life of the state. Hamilton immediately expressed his opposition to such an amendment, and he

146. Report on the Operation of the Act Laying Duties on Imports, Communicated to the House of Representatives on April 23, 1790, *Lodge*, II, 312.

made clear the manner of his reasoning which convinced him that the proposed amendment was unconstitutional. The principle, of course, of punishing privateers who fought for the British cause during the Revolution was right. Hamilton, however, was afraid that such a principle incorporated in the proposed amendment would punish "the innocent with the guilty," since many New York merchants during the war also had their vessels armed and were supplied with letters of marque. Thus, Hamilton continued the examination of the whole question "on the expediency and justice of the clause, distinct from constitutional considerations." His conclusion was that the amendment should be rejected, because by disfranchising the guilty, it could disfranchise at the same time the powerful class of the New York merchants. He ended his argument by asking: "Is it expedient to force, by exclusions and discriminations, a numerous and powerful class of citizens to be unfriendly to the government?"[147]

On another occasion, speaking on his financial policies and the reaction they produced, he stated that at an earlier stage there was "a similarity of thinking" between him and James Madison, which was relative "not merely to the general principles of national policy and government, but to the leading points, which were likely to constitute questions in the administration of finances. I mean, first, the expediency of funding the debt; second, the inexpediency of discrimination between original and present holders; third, the expediency of assuming the state debts.[148]

What Hamilton usually wanted to find out was the expediency of a principle, of a conclusion at which he had arrived or of measures that could make the enactment of a principle pos-

147. Speech in the New York Assembly, February 6, 1787, *Lodge*, VIII, 30.
148. Hamilton to Colonel Edward Carrington, Philadelphia, May 26, 1792, *Lodge*, IX, 514. See, also, *Lodge*, III, 298–99; IV, 74.

sible.[149] And the importance he attributed to "expediency" is evident in all instances where the process of his thought is clear. Moreover, it was not accidental that he often coupled "expediency" with highly respected qualities, as when he referred to the "wisdom and expediency of the plans,"[150] the "prudence and expediency,"[151] "expediency and justice,"[152] or "expediency and propriety,"[153] of measures and ideas.

"Expediency," according to Hamilton, was defined by circumstances. This is evident in statements such as, "the expediency of the measure must be tested by the state of things when it had its inception,"[154] or "The expediency of exercising a particular power, at a particular time, must, indeed, depend on circumstances."[155] These circumstances, of course, might be changed after a while and thus alter their relationship to the already defined expediency. Thus, after the new "state of things," a new expediency might emerge. Hamilton thought that since man is acting at a certain time, the circumstances of that time should be taken into consideration in defining "expediency."

This notion was of extreme importance for him, because, if the circumstances at a certain time made "inexpedient" the enactment of a conclusion or principle or even a single measure, one should abandon it; taking a "further step," constituted an

149. On Hamilton's inquiry on the expediency related to a measure see, for example, *Lodge*, II, 346; III, 46, 477; IV, 273; VI, 160; VII, 171, 217, 358; X, 256–57, 391.

150. "The Raynold's Pamphlet," *Lodge*, VII, 373.

151. "Report on Loans," *Lodge*, III, 150. "Camillus," No. 32, *Lodge*, VI, 120.

152. Speech in the New York Assembly, February 6, 1787, *Lodge*, VIII, 29.

153. Hamilton to Colonel Edward Carrington, *Lodge*, IX, 515; Hamilton to George Washington, November 18, 1799, *Lodge*, VII, 179.

154. "The Public Conduct and Character of John Adams, esq., President of the United States," *Lodge*, VII, 345.

155. Hamilton to George Washington, on the Constitutionality of the Bank of the United States, February 23, 1791, *Lodge*, III, 452.

"error."[156] On the contrary, if circumstances at a certain time indicated an "expediency," then one should act according to it. There was only one exception, a significant one, where "expediency" should be ignored; and this was when an issue of "right" was involved. Hamilton in this case did not make a distinction between right defined by a natural law and right framed by a positive law. He was simply explicit in his notion that if there was a question of right in general, expediency should yield. An analysis of this attitude of Hamilton makes it evident that he always made clear the distinction between "expediency" and "right." Giving, for instance, his opinion on the constitutionality of the Bank of the United States and answering various objections, he remarked: "Most of the arguments of the Secretary of State, which have not been considered in the foregoing remarks, are of a nature rather to apply to the expediency than to the constitutionality of the bill."[157] And further along, speaking on the same subject, he noted: "The quality of the object, as how far it will really promote or not the welfare of the Union, must be a matter of conscientious discretion, and the arguments for or against a measure in this light must be arguments concerning expediency or inexpediency, not constitutional right."[158] Again, discussing the attitude of the United States toward France in 1798, he clarified his position: "How far it may have been wise in a particular government to have taken up the gauntlet, or, if in its option, to have left France to the fermentations of the pernicious principles by which its leaders were actuated, is a question of mere expediency, distinct from the right."[159]

156. On "inexpedience" and "inexpedient" see, for example, *Lodge*, III, 462; IV, 269, 307–08, 309; VI, 477–78; VII, 40; VIII, 9, 111, 281, 341; IX, 191, 440; X, 325, 349.

157. Hamilton to George Washington, February 23, 1791, *Lodge*, III, 463.

158. *Lodge*, III, 485. See also, *ibid.*, 459.

159. "The Stand," April 4, 1798, *Lodge*, VI, 273. See also, Hamilton to Thomas Jefferson (Cabinet Paper), March 1792, *Lodge*, IV, 355; "Camillus," No. 32, 1795, *Lodge*, VI, 115–16.

Second, it becomes evident that though Hamilton had separated the notions of "expediency" and "right," he customarily gave due attention to both of them. In his examination of Jefferson's message to Congress of December 7, 1801, he stated: "Hitherto the proposal for sacrificing the internal revenue has been tried almost by the test of expediency; it is time to put it to a severe test—that of *right. Can the proposed abolition take effect without impairing the PUBLIC FAITH?*"[160]

Third, it is clear that when an issue of right or even moral obligation was involved, Hamilton endeavored to determine what was both right or morally obliging and, at the same time, what was expedient. Then he acted accordingly. Thus, in 1800, advocating the abolition of distinction between special compensations to persons not in the army and similar compensations to army officers for services which did not appertain to the nature of their offices, he stated: "There can be no doubt on this question where justice and expediency point."[161] And earlier, in his First Report on the Public Credit, he remarked: "While the observance of that good faith, which is the basis of public credit, is recommended by the strongest inducements of political expediency, it is enforced by considerations of still greater authority. There are arguments for it which rest on the immutable principles of moral obligation."[162]

In case expediency was contrary to what had been established as right, however, then he had to act according to the latter. In 1787, in the New York Assembly, attacking a principle introduced by a clause of an election bill which prohibited pensioners and officers under Congress from sitting in Assembly or Senate, Hamilton stated:

But I mean to lay honestly before you the dangers to which we expose ourselves by letting in the principle which the

160. Examination of Jefferson's Message to Congress of December 7, 1801, No. 4, December 26, 1801, *Lodge,* VIII, 265. Hamilton's emphasis.
161. Hamilton to Caleb Swan, May 26, 1800, *Lodge,* VII, 220.
162. "First Report on the Public Credit," *Lodge,* II, 230–31.

clause under consideration rests upon. I give no opinion on the expediency of the exclusion proposed. I only say, in my opinion the Constitution does not permit it, and I shall be against any qualification or disqualification—either of electors or elected—not prescribed by the Constitution."[163]

On another occasion, criticizing his fellow citizens who offended his sense of justice by overlooking the corruption and extortion of the French Directory, he condemned the support of a policy of compliance with the French demands:

And yet there are men, could it be believed, vile and degenerate enough to run about the streets to contradict, to palliate, to justify, to preach the expediency of compliance. Such men merit all the detestation of all their fellow citizens; there is no doubt that with time and opportunity they will merit much more from the offended justice of the laws.[164]

This exception of the prevalence of right over expediency was the only one admitted by Hamilton.[165] It was, perhaps, the result

163. Speech in the New York Assembly, January 27, 1787, *Lodge,* VIII, 27.

164. "The Stand," No. 5, April 16, 1798, *Lodge,* VI, 302.

165. Despite the fact that I intended to base this book wholly upon primary sources, I believe it "expedient" to refer to a remark of Parrington whose penetrating eye recognized the important role played by "expediency" in Hamilton's thought; and he is, perhaps, the only one who mentions it. *En passant,* Parrington notes: "The current Federalist dogma of the divine right of justice—*vox justiciae vox dei*—was at hand to serve his (Hamilton's) purpose and he made free use of it. But no ethical gilding could quite conceal a certain ruthlessness of purpose; in practice justice became synonymous with expediency, and expediency was curiously like sheer Tory will to power." And further along writing about the assumption of the public debt by the Federal Government, he states that Hamilton believed that: "The argument of expediency must prevail over abstract justice."—Vernon Louis Parrington, *Main Currents in American Thought* (New York, 1930), I, 300, 304. In the light of Hamilton's insistence that expediency should yield to justice, it is unfortunate that Parrington chose to phrase his comment in this way.

of his legalistic outlook and the impact upon him of the Natural Rights philosophy. In every other instance, however, where no explicit issue of right was involved, Hamilton attributed to expediency a grave importance.[166]

The relation of "expediency" to the problem of the validity of a principle (or maxim, or conclusion) which Hamilton could reach through a rational process is evident. One can clearly see that the correctness of such a principle depends not only upon the soundness and propriety of the empirical data on which the principle was founded, but also on the expediency of the principle's enactment. Thus, the authority of a principle, derived from proper facts, was greatly enlarged whenever circumstances required or suggested or made possible its practical application. And yet, expediency was not, for Hamilton, the last factor determining the validity of a principle. The latter should pass further, in the course of its enactment, through the stage of an "experiment," through the "test of the experience of the future," and it was this "test" that would finally show the merits of such a principle.

9. *"Nothing less than experimental certainty ought to have been relied upon."*

166. For more examples on the use of "expediency" by Hamilton see *Lodge*, II, 17, 44, 250, 296, 301, 325, 340; III, 118, 288; IV, 25, 39, 53, 58, 70, 131, 166, 172, 173, 288, 356, 357, 393; V, 17, 54, 134, 290, 393, 443; VI, 115, 334, 348; VII, 155, 222, 410; VIII, 29, 117, 126, 273, 298; IX, 110, 365, 536; X, 80, 177, 180, 304, 340, 425. For the use of "expedient" as an adjective and noun, and in the latter's double sense, that is either as the most suitable and/or profitable means for the accomplishment of an end, or simply as means, see, for example, *Lodge*, II, 275, 276, 280, 284, 364, 365, 390, 393, 400, 409–11; III, 101–02, 140, 194, 266, 274, 295, 302, 311, 324, 325, 332, 339, 370, 371, 373, 398, 417, 420, 422, 424, 443, 468, 475, 487; IV, 15, 44, 52, 54, 55, 72, 97, 116, 145, 147, 168, 180, 188, 233, 267, 275, 310, 325, 341, 350, 412, 427; V, 45, 68, 97, 119, 122, 204, 247, 277, 288, 374, 408, 445, 460; VI, 107, 245, 306, 320, 335, 341, 342, 367, 428, 431, 434, 484; VII, 5, 32, 39, 55, 64, 75, 78, 97, 149, 163, 169, 173, 176–77, 185, 223, 333, 395; VIII, 76, 124, 330, 342, 375, 483; IX, 5, 8, 20, 28, 147–48, 160, 319, 383, 454, 455, 486, 502, 504; X, 304, 19, 89, 175, 294, 314, 362, 375, 394, 403, 429, 430, 433.

"Experiment" is another term dearly cherished by Hamilton and repeatedly met in his writings. The notion of "experimental verification" occupied such an important place in Hamilton's philosophic method that a discussion of his mode of employment of it becomes necessary.

The word "experiment" appeared with several connotations in Hamilton's phraseology. Sometimes it meant a process for the factual verification of a certain conclusion. Thus, when in his *Report on Manufactures* Hamilton suggested measures for the protection of the country's distilleries, he concluded: "Experiment could, perhaps, alone decide with certainty the justness of the suggestions which are made."[167] Again, when in his *Report on Public Credit* Hamilton outlined a plan for the conversion of the whole foreign debt into a domestic one, he explained: "It has occurred that the present posture of the affairs of Europe might favor a plan of this kind, and perhaps produce some collateral advantages. Under this idea, an experiment is proposed."[168] Furthermore, criticizing Jefferson's Message to Congress of December 7, 1801, Hamilton attacked the President for his idea of relinquishing the internal revenue by arguing that there was "a reasonable ground of confidence that it may safely be dispensed with." Hamilton, on the contrary, defended his own principles by asking that their enactment, then in process "by way of experiment," decide their validity. In his words:

Nothing less than experimental certainty ought to have been relied upon. There was no pressure of circumstances making it proper to precipitate the measure. It would have been ridiculous to pretend that the burden is so heavy as to demand immediate relief; and without this incentive to relinquishment, experience ought undoubtedly to have been taken as the only fit and sure guide.

Not only is it problematical what the present duties on im-

167. "Report on Manufactures," *Lodge,* V, 177.
168. "Report on Public Credit," January 1795, *Lodge,* III, 260.

ports will for succeeding years produce; but it is in a degree questionable, whether it may not be found necessary to reduce the rates. That they are now high, when compared with the commercial capital of our country, is not to be denied, and whether they may not be found too high for a beneficial course of our trade, is yet to be decided by experiment. The latter augmentations of the rates of duty were made at times and under circumstances in the situations of this and of other countries, which forbid us to regard past experience as conclusive on the point.

Should it be said in answer, that the revenues can hereafter be renewed, if on trial it shall be found that they have been prematurely abandoned, the decisive reply is, that this is to invert the natural order of just reasoning. Were it now the question, whether such revenues should be created, in anticipation of a possible deficiency, the correct answer would be, let experiment first ascertain the necessity: as they already exist, on a question to abolish them, the answer equally ought to be, let experience first show them to be unnecessary.[169]

At other times, "experiment" meant an inquiry into the facts of a certain situation, which would lead to the discovery of a conclusion. Such was the case when, deeply concerned in fixing the length and "velocity" of the military pace Hamilton wrote:

I observe that the French regulations, as well as those of several other countries, adopt a *fixed* measure for the pace (pas), without regard to the velocity, which, in the French code, is *two feet French*. As the measures differ in different *European* establishments, I have been causing experiments to be made, in order to discover, if practicable, a standard in nature relatively to the medium size of a man. In the course of these experiments, it appears that though two feet is about the natural length of the cadenced step — say seventy-five in a minute — of a body of men, yet they naturally increase the length of the step with the velocity.

This has led me to some new reflections on the point; and as

169. Jefferson's Message, No. 2, *Lodge,* VIII, 255–56.

I respect European precedents, in a science which has been so much studied and practiced, I am desirous of knowing what reasoning has led to the adopting of a *determinate length* for all the direct steps, without regard to velocity — that is to say, the same for the quick and quickest.[170]

And writing on the same subject he elaborated:

But to arrive at a full result, it is necessary that the experiments should be multiplied, should be by individuals of different sizes, and by bodies of different numbers from few to many, and especially that they should be on different sorts of ground, rough as well as smooth, unequal as well as plain. By this diversification of the experiments, it may be possible to discover some medium which, being adopted as a standard, and made habitual to the troops, will best accommodate itself to the variety of circumstances which occur.[171]

Or, again, before the adoption by the army of a new type of rifle, the Ferguson, which had already been introduced in European armies as being more quickly loaded and more easily kept clean than were other rifles of the time, Hamilton thought that "if the shot of it be equally sure, or nearly so, those advantages entitle it to a preference. It is very desirable that this point, and its comparative merit in other respects, be ascertained by careful examination and experiment."[172]

In a third sense, Hamilton conceived "experiment" as a tentative policy or trial to discover the possibility of enacting a conclusion, and in case of a positive outcome, to determine the best way to make the enactment possible.

Thus, when in the spring of 1794 British-American relations were at a critical point and the threat of a war was imminent,

170. Hamilton to de Noailles, New York, May 5, 1800, *Lodge*, VII, 207. Hamilton's emphasis.

171. "The Step," 1800, *Lodge*, VII, 201–02.

172. Hamilton to George Washington (Cabinet Paper), April 14, 1794, *Lodge*, V, 98.

Hamilton explained the course that should be followed by the American Government:

> To take effectual measures of military preparation, creating, in earnest, force and revenue; to vest the President with important powers respecting navigation and commerce for ulterior contingencies — to endeavor by another effort of negotiation, confided to hands able to manage it, and friendly to the object, to obtain reparation for the wrongs we suffer, and a demarkation of a line of conduct to govern in future; to avoid till the issue of that experiment all measures of a nature to occasion a conflict between the motives which might dispose the British Government to do us the justice to which we are entitled and the scene of its own dignity. If that experiment fails, then and not till then to resort to reprisals and war.[173]

And further on, he repeated: "All ostensibly agree, that one more experiment of negotiation ought to precede actual war."[174] A few years later, in 1798, when a similar crisis erupted between the United States and France, Hamilton defended the policy of the American Government in maintaining peace. Explaining the situation, he recalled the American attempt to send General Pinckney as a Minister to France in order to seek a conciliation between the two countries. General Pinckney, however, had not been received by the French Government. And Hamilton continued:

> Though it was very problematical whether the honor of the United States, after this, permitted a further advance, yet the government, anxious if possible to preserve peace, concluded to make another and more solemn experiment. A new mission, confided to three extraordinary ministers, took place.[175]

Analyzing the financial situation of the United States in the year 1780, Hamilton remarked:

Paper credit never was long supported in any country, on a

173. *Lodge,* V, 98.
174. *Lodge,* V, 105.
175. "The Stand," No. 5, *Lodge,* VI, 300; see, also, "The Public Conduct and Character of John Adams," *Lodge,* VII, 329–30.

national scale, where it was not founded on a joint basis of public and private credit. An attempt to establish it on public credit alone in France, under the auspices of Mr. Law, had nearly ruined the kingdom. We have seen the effects of it in America, and every successive experiment proves the futility of the attempt.[176]

On several occasions he gave to "experiment" a fourth sense, that of an experience not purposely initiated, (as in the above cases), but one which happened to occur fortuitously so that, during the experience, a conscious observation of its process could take place and conclusions be reached. In this manner, Hamilton, in his famous letter in which he proposed the establishment of a military academy, although he advocated the union in it of the schools of engineers and artillerists, at the same time suggested the separation of the officers who were engineers and artillerists into two distinct corps.

This (the expediency of such separation) has been ascertained by experience. It is understood that one or more governments of Europe, particularly attentive to the military art, have essayed the union of the two corps, induced to it by their mutual relations in certain respects, and by the desire of insuring harmony in the service, and that the result of the experiment has led to a renunciation of the plan, as being productive of more disadvantages than advantages.

Influenced, as well by this experience in other countries as by my own observations and reflections, I beg leave to suggest for consideration a new arrangement on the subject, to be submitted, if approved, to the legislative body.[177]

At a much earlier period, in 1774, speaking on the beneficial results for England of her commerce with the American colonies, Hamilton remarked:

176. Hamilton to James Duane, September 3, 1780, *Lodge*, I, 233. See, also, *Lodge*, VII, 185.

177. Hamilton to McHenry, New York, November 23, 1799, *Lodge*, VII, 185.

The consumption of her manufactures in these colonies supplies the means of subsistence to a vast number of her most useful inhabitants. The experiment we have made heretofore shows us of how much importance our commercial connection is to her, and gives us the highest assurance of obtaining immediate redress by suspending it.[178]

It is remarkable how strongly the quest for "experimental certainty" was expressed by Hamilton and how frequently he resorted to it.[179] One more example will further clarify the place of "experiment" in Hamilton's method for acquiring knowledge.

The establishment of a National Bank was for the first time advocated by Hamilton in his well-known letter to General John Sullivan, in 1780. In this letter Hamilton did not resort to theoretic speculations on the subject, but offered a concrete plan of action. "If I offer anything new and useful," he wrote in it, "I am persuaded you will endeavor to turn it to advantage."[180] In this letter, after first examining the country's state of currency, he attacked the idea, expressed by several responsible men, that the situation could be resolved by domestic expedients and not by the procurement of a foreign loan. "This idea," he remarked, "proceeded from an ignorance of the real extent of our resources."[181] Subsequently, he continued with a factual analysis of the relationships between money and every branch of production in the country. He concluded: "The idea (that a foreign loan was not needed) was chimerical."[182]

178. "A Full Vindication," *Lodge,* I, 16–17.
179. For more examples on the use of "experiment" by Hamilton, see, *Lodge,* I, 203, 264; II, 42, 183, 210, 267, 281–82, 325, 340, 373–74, 398; III, 39, 63, 173, 305, 379, 398, 419, 442; IV, 9, 40, 43, 105, 181, 251, 273, 428; V, 176, 209–10, 243, 278, 316, 447; VI, 400, 403, 404–07, 416, 439; VII, 34, 195, 272, 330; VIII, 10–11, 36, 43–44, 239, 240, 313, 470; IX, 310, 315–16, 320, 341, 390, 419–20, 449; X, 16, 30, 181, 194, 341, 368, 447, 448.
180. Hamilton to General John Sullivan (Lodge mistakenly thought that it was addressed to Robert Morris), 1780, *Lodge,* III, 320.
181. Hamilton to Sullivan, *Lodge,* III, 320.
182. *Lodge,* III, 322.

He further explained his "reasonings" which emphasized American experience with the relation between commerce and currency, as well as the experiences with the same subject on the part of Russia, Prussia, Denmark, Sweden and especially the United Provinces. "From these reasonings it results," he maintained, that it was not in the power of Congress to prevent the depreciation of money. "There was but one remedy: a foreign loan."[183]

When he had reached this conclusion and established not only the expediency, but also the necessity for a foreign loan, he asked: "How this loan is to be employed is now the question."[184] In order to give an answer to it, he first examined two plans that had been proposed by others. He projected them against the background of American conditions, especially those of the farmers, who constituted the majority of the population and to whom both plans primarily appealed; and he also related the plans to the people's pattern of reactions in financial matters. He found that both plans had some merits, but as a whole they could not be effective in bringing the desired results. They both included several defective aspects, the most serious, in his opinion, being that they were not entirely founded on reality. He remarked:

> A great source of error in disquisitions of this nature, is the judging of events by abstract calculations; which, though geometrically true, are false as they relate to the concerns of beings governed more by passion and prejudice than by an enlightened sense of their interests. A degree of illusion mixes itself in all the affairs of society.[185]

Since psychological reactions, which definitely constitute part of the reality, had not been taken into consideration in those two plans, Hamilton thought that errors in them were inevitable.

He then endeavored to find the meaning of the already ana-

183. *Lodge*, III, 224–25.
184. *Lodge*, III, 226.
185. *Lodge*, III, 328.

lyzed facts, and when he achieved a synthesis, he was led to the conclusion that such a plan would not necessarily appeal to farmers; on the contrary: "The only plan that can preserve the currency is one that will make it the *immediate* interest of the moneyed men to co-operate with government in its support."[186] Expressing his plan in practical terms, he therefore recommended: "Article I. The plan I would propose is that of an American bank, instituted by authority of Congress for ten years, under the denomination of the Bank of the United States."[187] And he proceeded with the description of the main features of such an institution.

The principle of establishing a National Bank seemed to him very sound; the facts that supported such an establishment were numerous and convincing; while, at the same time, circumstances suggested its expediency. Such a bank, however, was a "novelty" for the country; it lacked the test of experience. For this reason he proposed its establishment on an experimental basis, that is, for ten years. Hamilton explained:

I have confined the bank to the space of ten years, because this will be long enough to judge of its advantages and disadvantages; and the latter may be rectified by giving it a new form. I do not suppose it will ever be discontinued; because it seems to be founded on principles that must always operate well, and make it the interest, both of government and the company, to uphold it. But I suppose the plan capable of improvement, which experience will suggest.[188]

A year later, on April 30, 1781, Hamilton sent a larger and more detailed letter on the same subject, virtually a treatise, to Robert Morris. He followed in it the same thread of thought expressed in the letter to Sullivan, only now he made a better analysis of the domestic experience, with more data on the financial situation of certain large states and a deeper insight into the

186. *Lodge*, III, 332. Hamilton's emphasis.
187. *Lodge*, III, 333.
188. *Lodge*, III, 339–40.

country's commercial situation. This time, also, Hamilton utilized foreign experience more thoroughly, adding France and England to the countries discussed in his Sullivan letter. The empirical data led him to conclude that a plan was needed which would solve the currency crisis, secure the independence of the country, promote commerce and be a source of national strength and wealth. To make clear his conclusions he stated: "I mean the institution of a NATIONAL BANK,"[189] and he wrote it with capital letters.

He then proceeded with a general outline of a proposed organization for the Bank in twenty articles. There one finds: "Article XVII. The bank to be established for thirty years by way of experiment."[190] And he justified this provision in a manner similar to that in his letter to General Sullivan.

In 1790, when Hamilton submitted his "Report on the National Bank" to the House of Representatives, he omitted a clause suggesting an experiment. The Bank this time had a permanent outlook. Perhaps the reason for the omission was that during the nine years that had passed since his letter to Robert Morris a great change had taken place and new problems had appeared. The war was over; the United States had become an independent country; pressing domestic problems, such as the economic recovery of the country and solution to the thorny question of the public debt, required permanency in the proposed measures; moreover, three banks existed already in the United States, and one of them, the Bank of North America, had for years a direct relation to the Government of the country.[191] A keen observation and a thorough study of banking experience abroad had proved that national banks had gained wide acceptance:

It is a fact, well understood, that public banks have found admission and patronage among the principal and most en-

189. Hamilton to Robert Morris, April 30, 1781, *Lodge,* III, 360.
190. *Lodge,* III, 379.
191. *Lodge,* III, 415.

lightened commercial nations. They have successively obtained in Italy, Germany, Holland, England, and France, as well as in the United States . . . there exists not a question about their utility in the countries in which they have been so long established. Theorists and men of business unite in acknowledgment of it.[192]

Thus, Hamilton concluded that there had been enough experience on this matter. No further experiment was needed.

10. *The Provisional Character of Hamilton's Principles.*

The relationship between "experiment" and "principle" in the process of Hamilton's thought was of utmost importance. The validity of a principle or conclusion at which Hamilton had arrived through an analysis and synthesis of empirical data depended not only on the soundness and propriety of these data and on the expediency of enactment, but also on experimental verification. It was the "experiment" that permitted a scientific verification of a principle or conclusion, demonstrating, at the same time, practical consequences, and essentially contributing to the acquisition of knowledge.

Instead of arriving, by means of a rational process, at an absolute principle, unchangeable and static, not capable of further development, Hamilton attained a provisional principle which, itself, could be used afresh as a foundation and a new starting point for further reasonings. True, such a principle was then deprived of the Olympian magnificence of an absolute authority and eternal value, but it was thoroughly dynamic, offering endless possibilities, and demonstrating the progressive utility of reason.

It should be remarked that Hamilton had a very clear notion of the provisional quality of his principles. He knew that the authority of most of them extended over a well-defined area, that they were founded on limited experience and concerned only one or a small number of topics. Hamilton, in fact, went so far that even "general principles," such as those referring to the law

192. *Lodge,* III, 389.

of nations to which he usually attributed a catholic validity were frequently subjected to "exceptions." For instance, in the course of defending his funding system, he came across one of those principles:

> The principle which shall be assumed here is this, that the established *rules of morality and justice are applicable to nations as well as individuals;* that the *former* as well as the *latter* are bound *to keep their promises; to fulfill their engagements to respect the rights of property* which others have acquired under contracts with them.[193]

And then he pointed out that to this principle there were certain exceptions according to which a nation or individual could violate its promises. He defined these exceptions as follows:

> The characteristics of the only admissable exceptions to the principle that has been assumed are — 1st, NECESSITY. 2nd, There being some intrinsic and inherent quality in the thing which is to constitute the exception, contrary to the social order and to the permanent good of society. Necessity is admitted in all moral reasoning as an exception to general rules. It is of two kinds, as applied to nations — where there is want of ability to perform a duty, and then it is involuntary; and where the general rule cannot be observed without some *manifest* and *great* national calamity.[194]

Thus, the inability of one of the involved parties, could constitute sound grounds on which this party could refrain from performing his duty. "But the inability must be a real, not a pretended one; one that has been experimentally ascertained, or that can be demonstrated to the satisfaction of all honest and discerning men."[195] He warned that although there were exceptions to the

193. "Vindication of the Funding System," No. 3, 1791, *Lodge,* III, 13. Hamilton's emphasis.

194. *Lodge,* III, 15. Hamilton's emphasis.

195. *Lodge,* III, 15. A similar view has been expressed by Hamilton concerning "extreme necessity," in *Lodge,* VIII, 43–44; for "necessity," especially in its relationship to "expediency," see *Lodge,* III, 229, 459; VIII, 126–27, 273, 355.

general principles, people should be very careful in admitting exceptions because: "The admission of them is one of the most common as well as the most fruitful sources of error and abuse, it is of the greatest importance that just ideas should be formed of their true nature, foundation, and extent."[196]

On another occasion when Hamilton was examining the impact of duties laid upon imports by various states on the balance of trade among the states in general, he remarked: "Between separate nations this reasoning will not apply with full force, because a multitude of local and extraneous circumstances may counteract the principle." And after elaborating on this statement, he continued: "General principles in subjects of this nature ought always to be advanced with caution; in an experimental analysis there are found such a number of exceptions as tend to render them very doubtful."[197] Once Hamilton had admitted that there were exceptions to the rules established by "general" principles, he rendered the latter's absolute character "very doubtful" indeed.

However, a principle, provisional as it could be, was highly esteemed by Hamilton. It should be remembered that the knowing process could start either from an accumulated number of empirical data, or from principles, or from both. Thus, on one occasion, Hamilton claimed that his reasoning was just, because "this is reasoning from the plainest principles."[198] Another time he attacked his opponents because their reasoning was "not supported by principle or fact; that (was) mere verbiage and idle declamation."[199] And again in a similar situation, he stated:

This is an argument of possibility and chance — one that would render useless all reasonings upon probable operation of things, and defeat the established principles of natural and moral causes. It is a species of reasoning sometimes used to excite popular jealousies, but is generally discarded by wise and discerning men.[200]

196. *Lodge*, III, 14.
197. "The Continentalist," No. 5, April 18, 1782, *Lodge*, I, 275.
198. Convention of New York, June 25, 1788, *Lodge*, II, 55.
199. Convention of New York, June 25, 1788, *Lodge*, II, 63.
200. *Lodge*, II, 37.

His esteem, however, toward the role dramatized by principles was better expressed when he declared:

> In reasoning upon all subjects, it is necessary to take as a point of departure, some principle in which reasonable and sound minds will agree. Without this there can be no argument, no conclusion, in moral or political more than in physical or mathematical disquisitions.[201]

11. *The Pragmatic Notions in Hamilton's Thought*

A great number of students of Hamilton's life, fascinated by his colorful and controversial personality, fail to penetrate beneath the surface of his statements and hence are ready to deny that his mind functioned in response to a "philosophy." They probably remember that Hamilton had attacked Hobbes,[202] had called Spinoza "a celebrated sophist,"[203] had repeatedly expressed a deep respect for Hume, though his references were to the latter's economic essay only,[204] and had admired Grotius, Vattel and many other exponents of Natural Rights philosophy.[205] But since these are not enough to make him a disciple of any philosophic system, it is convenient to conclude that every attempt of Hamilton to "philosophize" merely reflected his verve for polemics, his argumentative techniques and his tendency to display erudition.

To a limited extent these scholars are correct. It is impossible to trace a consistent philosophic system in Hamilton's thought. For he was a typical man of the Enlightenment, a fact—and this is important—which he well knew.[206] A closed, well-defined philosophic system, with its crystallized doctrines or dogmas, offering

201. "Vindication of the Funding System," No. 3, 1791, *Lodge*, III, 13.
202. *Lodge*, I, 61–62.
203. *Lodge*, I, 83.
204. *Lodge*, I, 72–74, 81, 269–70, 412; III, 346; VII, 406; IX, 551.
205. *Supra*, fn. No. 107.
206. For Hamilton's references to "this enlightened age," and in general his use of the term "enlightened," see, for example, *Lodge*, I, 61; II, 346; III, 361, 384, 389; IV, 284; V, 234; VII, 330.

a stratospheric view to earthly realities below, could not give Hamilton the freedom he wanted, the method he needed to understand the realities in the midst of which he was volcanically active, of which he was dynamically a part. Thus, one cannot find in him an *esprit de système*. What one clearly finds in his mind, forcefully projected, constantly and with consequence from the moment he appeared very early as a public figure up to his death,[207] is an *esprit systématique*.

Ernest Cassirer has already convincingly shown that this was the characteristic of all typical thinkers of the Enlightenment.[208] However, Hamilton was somewhat different from many of his contemporary thinkers in the greater use of what has been called pragmatic notions. Students who fail to discern these notions and to assign their significant place in Hamilton's knowing process, commit grave mistakes. Most of the misunderstandings related to Hamilton, (with the exception of those which give evidence of deeply-rooted auctorial prejudices), are due to an ignorance of Hamilton's pattern of thought. To illustrate this statement one could employ a great number of examples; two, however, will suffice.

In a review of two new additions to Hamiltoniana during the celebration of Hamilton's Bicentennial Year, a reviewer said: "Of course, no world was ever made for Hamilton. He was a

207. This does not mean, however, that Hamilton's intellectual outlook remained static for almost thirty years. The reader of Hamilton is soon convinced of the contrary and can readily note the greater maturity and enrichment of Hamilton's thought in his later years, as well as his expanded powers of analysis and synthesis. This book is primarily concerned, however, not with the whole intellectual world of Hamilton, but simply with his epistemology. Even here and within the frame of an *esprit systématique*, a certain development occurred. This can be traced in this study through the dates added to the various references and there, for instance, one can note that as Hamilton grew older, the pragmatic strain of his mind gained ascendance at the expense of his allegiance to Natural Rights concepts.

208. Ernest Cassirer, *The Philosophy of the Englihtenment*, translated by Fritz C. A. Koelin and James P. Pettergrove (Princeton, New Jersey, 1951).

dreamer, not a realist; he lived in plans and hopes."[209] No matter what the literary merits of such a statement, after the preceding analysis of Hamilton's thought, one thing is clear—this statement is inaccurate.

In another, otherwise brilliant study, the author uses almost four pages pointing out "contradictions and inconsistencies" of Hamilton, showing that on one occasion he supported one policy, or idea, and on another he supported some measure different if not opposite to, his previous views.[210] The account is accurate, but its author failed to understand Hamilton's pragmatic approach. He failed to see that for Hamilton an achieved conclusion had not an unchangeable but a provisional character; that every question was approached by him as a distinct and separate case; that changing circumstances could define a different kind of expediency. In short, an ignorance of Hamilton's pragmatic notions by the author made him fail to explain why these "contradictions and inconsistencies" occurred.

When we take into consideration the degree of Hamilton's reliance on experience, his distrust of abstractions, his concern with the "practicability" of things,[211] his experimentalism and all the pragmatic strains in his thought which were previously discussed, we are inclined to consider him as a pragmatist. William James affirmed that a pragmatist is one who

> turns his back resolutely and once for all upon a lot of inveterate habits dear to professional philosophers. He turns away from abstraction and insufficiency, from verbal solutions, from bad *a priori* reasons, from fixed principles, closed systems, and

209. J. H. Powell, "Two New Studies of Alexander Hamilton," *Saturday Review* (January 19, 1957), p. 38.

210. Joseph Charles, "Hamilton and Washington: The Origins of the American Party System," *The William and Mary Quarterly*, XII, No. 2, third series (April 1955), 221–24.

211. On Hamilton's quest for "practicability," as well as "utility" see, for example, *Lodge*, II, 30; III, 29, 102, 229, 425, 488; IV, 39, 115, 125; VI, 335, 407; VII, 207; VIII, 11; IX, 420; X, 425, 433.

pretended absolutes and origins. He turns toward concreteness and adequacy, towards facts, towards action and towards power. That means the empiricist temper regnant and the rationalist temper sincerely given up. It means the open air and possibilities of nature, as against dogma, artificiality, and the pretense of finality in truth.[212]

This definition fits Hamilton comfortably, but not completely. A disciple of William James would face a dilemma as to whether he should consider Hamilton a pragmatist. The reason is that "the rationalist temper is not entirely given up." Few as they were, there were still cases where Hamilton resorted through the Natural Rights philosophy to those "bad *a priori* reasons."

On the other hand, the same disciple would observe that by following a psychological approach and taking into consideration Hamilton's "will to believe" in the immutability of Natural Rights; by considering the practical consequences which this belief had on Hamilton's conduct and behavior, on his morale and determination during the Revolution and on his confidence and certainty of outlook in cases concerning international relations as an absolute quality in the actualities which Hamilton experienced, one would probably find that there is nothing wrong in granting Hamilton a place among the pragmatists. And though this study does not aim to make Hamilton fit a certain pattern or classification, it has to agree with such a conclusion: Hamilton indeed was a pragmatist *sui generis;* and the way to understand his mind clearly is to acknowledge its strong pragmatic bent.

212. William James, *Pragmatism* (New York, 1908), 51.

Index

Adams, John, 77, fn. 20; 79; 91, fn. 116; 103, fn. 154; 111, fn. 175
Aeschylus, 10
Aesop, 10
America, 36, 73, **75**
American Revolution, 2, 89, 123
Americanus, 86, fn. 81; 91, fn. 118
Amianthus, 7, 39–40
Amphictyonic Council, **97, 100**
Aristotle, 8, 10, 41, 54
Asia, 36
Asia Minor, 25–26
Asia Minor Islands, 37–39
Austria, 33
Azores, 41

Baltic, 29
Barber, Francis, 10
Barnard, Sir John, ix, x
Bayard, James A., 78, fn. 42
Blackstone, 85, 90
Bohemia, 34–35
Breslau, Silesia, 9, **67**
Burlemaqui, 90
Bynkershoek, 90

Camillus, 76, fns. 6, **16**; **77, fn. 22**; 79, fn. 45; 84, fns. 71, 76; 87, fn. 82; 88, fn. 91; 89, fns. 97, 99, 102, 104; 94, fn. 128; 97, fn. 135; 99, fn. 140; 103, fn. 151; 104, fn. 159

Canaries, 41
Carrington, Col. Edward, 81, fn. 56; 102, fn. 148; 103, fn. 153
Cassirer, Ernest, 121
Catullus, 82, fn. 62
China, 36–37, 42
Cicero, 9, 10
Civis to Mercator, 80, fn. 50; 100, fn. 143
Clinton, Gov. George, 20; 78, fn. 36
Coin, 7, 8
Common-sense: Hamilton's notion of cf. 87–88
Continentalist, The, 9, fn. 16; 17; 18, fn. 38; 75, fns. 2, 3; 76, fn. 17; 77, fns. 20, 26; 78, fn. 43; 98, fn. 137; 119, fn. 197
Croswell, Harry, 87, fn. 83; 91, fn. 110
Cudworth, Ralph, 13

Davenant, 41
Demosthenes, 9, 12, 13, 45
Denmark, 30, 114
De Noailles, 110, fn. 170
De Witt, 24
Dionysius of Halicarnassus, 10
Duane, James, 112, fn. 176

125

Edited by Ita Kanter
Cover designed by Richard Berube
Set in Linotype Caledonia
and Commercial Script
Printed on Doeskin Offset and
bound in Sorg Plate Cover
Manufactured in the United States of America